WHAT
GROWS
TOGETHER

In loving memory of my Grandma, who introduced me to the real purpose of a garden: to be enjoyed and preferably with a large glass of something cold.

WHAT GROWS TOGETHER

JAMIE BUTTERWORTH

FAIL-SAFE PLANT COMBINATIONS FOR EVERY GARDEN

CONTENTS

6	Introduction
10	The Garden Shed
13	Plant Names and Types
16	Choosing and Caring for Your Plants
20	Designing a Combination

26	**Spring**
76	**Summer**
154	**Autumn**

200	Plant Combination Guide
216	Resources
216	Index
222	Acknowledgments
224	About the Author

Have you ever stood in a garden centre, overwhelmed by the choice, with hundreds of different plants, all with fancy Latin names and unfamiliar technical information? What starts off as a well-intentioned day out, with aspirations of reigniting your unloved garden, can result in you leaving £100 poorer with a tray of pansies and some plants you've never heard of before in full flower – only to discover they don't work well together, and rapidly die. An experience like this can be off-putting, the antithesis of why we garden and of the joy a garden can bring. But this book is here to help you make the right choices, and to create long-lasting displays throughout the year.

Gardening can be uplifting, inspiring, relaxing, and comforting – a way to make your home more beautiful and improve your mental health in the process. It's an escape from the daily grind that enables you to unwind in a haven of your own making. I strongly believe that you don't need to be a horticultural expert to create a personalized garden paradise, and, with over 15 years working in nurseries and gardens and designing with plants, I have learnt how to put together the most desirable combinations for all environments, using plants you can get hold of in any garden centre or online. This takes the tricky choices away, and maximizes your time, space, and hard-earned money.

This book is made up of over 60 different plant combinations, at their best from spring to autumn, though many offer year-round interest. Regardless of the size of your garden, knowledge, or budget, these simple-to-create plant "recipes" will ensure you never again feel overwhelmed when visiting the garden centre or planning your garden. There will be no horticultural jargon, no lecturing about how to do things, just good quality, beautiful combinations of easy-to-grow plants.

I have tried, tested, and grown all of these combinations, working out which plants grow well together (and most importantly look good together). While these combinations are appealing, straightforward to create, and simple to maintain, they are by no means rigid. I would encourage you to adapt and personalize them, to use them as a starting point. If you have a desire to add a bunch of bright pink *Dianthus*, or a splash of yellow sunflowers, then go for it! When cooking, I find it almost impossible to stick to the recipe, moving away from the instructions to adapt it more to my taste – this is no different.

The eagle-eyed among you may notice I have almost entirely avoided winter in this book – this wasn't an accident. By all means use the garden as an escape during these short winter days, but don't feel pressured into getting out there when it's blowing a gale. Increasingly, with winter being wetter, it is actually advisable to avoid planting anything in the deepest winter months. Let the ground dry out and the sun come out, and you will enjoy the garden a lot more – and so will your plants.

PLANTING LOCATIONS

For all my adult life, I have lived in rented accommodation; in common with many people, affording a house with my own garden is an unrealistic aspiration. I have learnt to adapt the way I garden, and to be creative with the often-limited space I have.

All of the combinations in this book can be adapted for any location, in the ground or in a container, whether you have a small balcony, a courtyard, or are lucky enough to have a larger garden. There's no need to be limited by the size of your space.

For each recipe, I indicate where best to position the plants so that they perform as well as possible. Simply keep an eye on how much sun you do (or don't) get, and check against the growing conditions advised for each recipe to ensure the plants will be happy in your garden. The detailed plant combination guide on pages 202–13 gives you all the information you need for each plant and grouping.

Inevitably some will be happier in your conditions than others – don't let that put you off. Some plants will die, others will thrive. It's all part of the process and should be celebrated. The journey to create these combinations can be as enjoyable as it is to see them flourishing in your garden.

THE GARDEN SHED

I am a firm believer that it takes just a few simple items and plants to create beautiful garden combinations. The tools, equipment, and materials covered here can be used in all recipes in this book and are widely available from any garden centre or DIY store, or online. These materials are to the garden what your utensils and store cupboard essentials are to the kitchen.

TROWEL OR SPADE

Depending on whether you are planting in containers or in the ground, you will need some form of tool to get your plants into their new home. A trowel is ideal for a container. A spade works in bigger areas: a good spade should go through ground like a knife through butter and make light work of planting your new plants.

CUTTING TOOLS

You will need to maintain your plant combinations. This may sound like a chore, but I promise you when your garden starts to come to life and you can see the beauty in it, maintaining your combinations will become a joy (see pp.18–19). Taking ten minutes out of your day every now and then to tend to your plants will become part of your routine.

Secateurs, snips, or scissors may soon be your new best friend. They vary in price from a couple of pounds to over £60 and, when you are ready to, I would highly recommend investing in a good quality pair that will see you through your gardening journey. But, to start with, a cheaper pair will do the job. You will use these for everything from deadheading to cutting flowering stems to create a bouquet of your lovely new plants, to trimming and chopping back to the ground for the winter (don't worry, I'll tell you which ones to cut and when to do it).

From time to time you may need something slightly bigger than secateurs to remove a larger branch from a shrub or tree. For this, I prefer to use a folding saw, nothing too big. Some people prefer loppers, but I find they can chew the bark rather than cut through it.

Lastly, if you are creating topiary or looking to shape any shrubs or plants, you may need a pair of shears. Again, I much prefer smaller and more nimble shears over large, heavy ones.

COMPOST

Often when you visit a garden centre you can be overwhelmed not just by the number and varieties of plants, but also the abundance of different composts. Unless you are running a commercial nursery it's hard to understand why you may need so many – and you don't. Quite truthfully, they're all much the same, just different brands. Don't worry about buying specialist composts – just go for a good quality, general multipurpose one. However, make sure the compost you are buying is peat free. In recent years peat-free composts have become the norm, so this shouldn't be hard, and it means you can garden knowing that your compost hasn't been dug up from precious peat bogs.

Regardless of whether you are planting in containers or garden borders, a good general multipurpose compost can be used for any

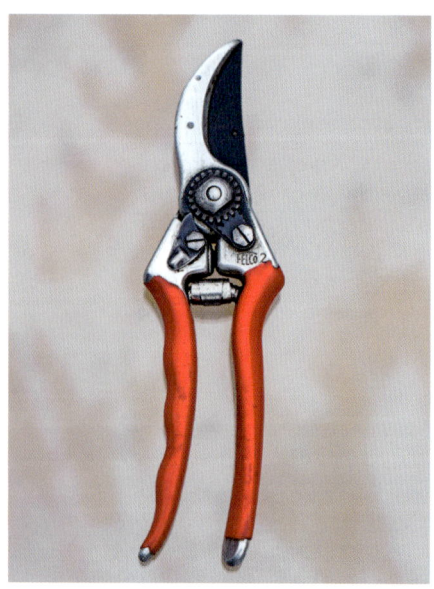

of these combinations. For container planting, the compost will fill your pots. If you're planting straight into the garden, you can improve the soil slightly with some of the compost to give the plants a good start.

WATER

Without stating the obvious, you will require access to water for these combinations to grow. It's quite staggering the number of times I've seen gardens without a tap – many new-build houses deem this an unnecessary addition. Even the most resilient combinations in this book need watering. This can be via a hose pipe, watering can, or even a jug – just make sure you can get water to your new plants.

POTS

All the combinations in this book can be grown in pots and containers as well as directly in a bed in the garden. Indeed, for the making of this book, all the combinations have been grown in a container. The type of container you use is entirely up to you. Whether it's a classical terracotta pot, a contemporary porcelain container, or quite frankly an old bathtub, it really doesn't matter so long as it has drainage holes in the bottom.

FERTILIZER

Another overwhelming part of any garden centre is its fertilizer section. I think you can never go wrong with a seaweed-based fertilizer – it is the only type I use at home. It comes in liquid form so you can add it when watering plants, it's almost impossible to use too much, yet the impact it will have is astronomical. Being seaweed derived, it's completely organic and harmless to the environment.

COMBINATION 43

PLANT NAMES AND TYPES

Plants are categorized into certain types according to how long they live and how they grow. I know, I promised I wouldn't use any horticultural jargon or fancy words. But there are a few words and descriptions that crop up from time to time, and I wanted to elaborate a little on what they mean.

PERENNIALS

A perennial is a plant that comes back year after year. Perennials are a brilliantly cost-effective way of planting up a garden, avoiding the need to replace or supplement plants each year. Herbaceous perennials typically die back in the winter and regenerate from the ground again the following spring. Many have a lifespan of around four to five years before they become tired. While this is a lot of value for a plant likely to cost you less than a tenner, you can extend their lifespan further by dividing the plants (see pp.18–19).

ANNUALS

An annual is a plant that germinates from seed, flowers, produces seed, and dies all within the same year. Annuals are typically cheap to buy, easy to grow, and provide fleeting moments of happiness that can add a sprinkling of magic into a garden. They are often purchased as seeds, which cost pennies in relative terms for the amount of potential plants you get (and that's what a seed is: a potential plant). You can also buy annuals as plug plants: tiny seedlings that have already germinated, and that will quickly grow into a larger plant, creating a quicker display. But honestly, what could be simpler than emptying out a seed packet among your plants and knowing you grew them yourself while saving yourself a fortune? Throughout this book, I encourage you to freely add annuals to the combinations to provide additional colour suited to your own tastes. From cosmos to cornflowers, sweet peas to sunflowers, there are thousands of incredible annuals for any garden.

ORNAMENTAL GRASSES

Grasses are plants that don't produce obvious flowers. Instead, they provide us with texture, movement, and structure – essential ingredients. Many have a similar lifespan to other perennials and also die back in the winter before regenerating the following spring.

BULBS

Emerging daffodils signal the start of spring: longer, warmer days, and the joy of being able to get back out into the garden more often. Bulbs are very possibly the best value for money you will spend in your garden. In autumn and early winter, you can buy and plant your bulbs for the following spring. My one rule is to always buy as many as you can afford. They (mostly) come back every year, and can be planted by simply pushing the bulbs into the ground. In some combinations I recommend certain bulbs that would work well, but ultimately, you can be creative with any of the combinations in this book.

TREES

Planting a tree is one of the best things you can do for your garden and the environment. In most cases you are going to be planting a small tree that doesn't come close to resembling its mature form. I use many trees throughout this book, but I have been quite careful about those I have chosen. Most are slower growing and unlikely to reach large sizes, so they can be easily managed, pruned, and controlled to keep their size and shape relative to the space you have. In many of the gardens I create, I use trees to provide the structure, architecture, and form – to hold the space together. Their woody branches and characterful trunks can be considered sculptures, negating the need for hard landscaping or built structures: trees will do all that for you at a fraction of the price.

SHRUBS

Smaller than a tree, larger than a perennial, these woody plants can also be used to create structure and introduce form to a space, but without growing as large as a tree. So they're ideal for smaller gardens, or for underplanting trees where you have a garden big enough.

TOPIARY

To topiarize a plant (usually a tree or shrub) is to clip it into a shape in which it wouldn't naturally grow. This could be anything from a ball, cone, dome, or pyramid to a life-sized horse. While I am normally a strong advocate for letting plants and gardens be naturalistic, there can be something very pleasing about topiarized shapes dotted through swathes of grasses and perennials. You can purchase ready-made topiary, and all you need to do is keep trimming it to its prescribed shape, or you can create your own by carefully pruning over a number of years. Each time you cut a stem, it will produce several more shoots, so in just a few years you can end up with a dense and defined shape.

PLANT NAMES Names of plants can be daunting, especially those long-winded Latin ones. To help keep things as simple as possible, we have used both Latin and common names, with the most colloquial version in the main text – and it's entirely up to you which you prefer to use. We also have included a Plant Combination Guide at the rear of the book from page 200 with all the growing information for each plant.

COMBINATION 47

AGM Many of the plants used throughout this book have "AGM" next to them. This stands for the Award of Garden Merit, given by the Royal Horticultural Society (RHS) to plants that they deem to be extremely strong performers. A panel of horticultural experts considers many different aspects of the plant's growth, flowering, availability, and much more before making the award. In a nutshell, when you see the AGM logo, you can be sure you are buying a proven strong grower that is likely to perform well.

PFP Another award given by the talented and clever folk at the RHS, this award stands for Plants for Pollinators. While our gardens are there to provide us with joy and beauty throughout the year, domestic gardens are also an essential habitat and food source for so many pollinators, which are fast dwindling in numbers. By actively choosing PFP plants, we can encourage more butterflies, bees, and other essential and beautiful insects to share our gardens.

CHOOSING AND CARING FOR YOUR PLANTS

You will find a lot more on how I have chosen the plants for the combinations in this book on the Designing pages that follow (see pp.20–25). Here I cover the practicalities of how to choose a healthy plant, how to settle it in its new home in the ground or in a pot, and how to look after it so it thrives.

CHOOSING A HEALTHY PLANT

Although it's possible to buy just about any plant online, I much prefer to visit a garden centre or nursery in person to hand select the very best plants. I'm always looking for the best of the batch, as getting a healthy plant to start with makes life much easier in the long run. You are looking for healthy foliage (no diseases, evidence of pest damage, marks, or discolouration), and a strong root system (when you take the plant out of the pot, healthy, white roots are visible, see photo, right). There is little difference, other than patience and budget, in opting for a large instant specimen or starting small.

TREES

A tree is an investment. Its true rewards will only really be felt or seen after a decade or longer, and it will most likely outlive you or me. Use what you can afford to get the best tree possible. It is much easier to start with a good shape, so visit a local grower, and hand choose your tree. Touch it, feel it, and find what you like best. Trees with multiple stems are my personal favourite, as they add real form to your outdoor space, showing off the character and shape of the tree while maintaining a view through the tree and allowing ample space for underplanting (see also p.23).

PLANTING

Whether it's a tree or a smaller perennial, planting couldn't be simpler: dig a hole and plop in the plant (or bulb, see left). As long as you get it the right way up, the plant will find a way to get going. If it's pot bound, with tightly packed roots circling inside the pot, you can gently tease out the roots (see right).

For most of the combinations in this book, it can take a year or more for them to truly start to mingle and fill out. In their first year after being planted, they need to take time to root, establish, and grow. That's OK. Don't worry if there are some gaps between the plants where you can see a little soil – they will soon cover this.

If you are impatient (as I am), you can use some annuals sprinkled among the plants. These will be quick to germinate, grow, and flower. Simply buy these as seeds and scatter them, following the timings on the packet. Bulbs are also easy to plant (see left) and can fill gaps and add seasonal colour.

In the top tips for various combinations, I have suggested some annuals and bulbs you could add that work well.

LOOKING AFTER YOUR PLANTS

There are a few things you need to do throughout the year to maximize your plants' health and performance and to achieve the best results.

WINTER STRUCTURE

For me, there is real beauty in seeing plants transform in winter. Foliage, seedheads, and old flowers turn crispy after they are struck by the first hard frost of the year, which is nature's way of bringing the growing season to an abrupt end. Leaving these plants in situ is not only brilliant as shelter and food for pollinators and other insects and wildlife, but they also look amazing. The frost dances off them on cold mornings, and even the way morning dew settles upon the old foliage can be mesmerizing.

DEADHEADING, CUTTING BACK, AND PRUNING

A very simple way of getting your flowering plants to flower longer, and better, is by deadheading. Simply snip off fading flowers. By removing them before they have had chance to develop into seeds, you will force the plant into sending out more and more flowers.

Many of the plants in this book need cutting back at the end of winter. Cut them to the ground using sharp secateurs or shears (see opposite, where I'm cutting back grasses in winter). The plants will regrow from their roots and offer fresh growth in spring. I have included advice on how to do this under combinations where it's relevant.

Trees, shrubs, and larger woodier plants with a permanent branch framework need pruning to keep the plant healthy and sometimes to shape it. Start with the four Ds: dead, diseased, damaged, and duplicated. Cut out any branches that are dead or showing signs of disease using sharp secateurs (see top, left), or a folding saw for thicker branches. Damaged branches can provide an access point for disease so need to go. Any branches that are crossing or rubbing can also be removed; take out the least vigorous of the two.

You don't want to remove more than one-third of the tree or shrub in one go, so if by doing the above you have already removed quite a lot, leave it for another year. If you have removed less than one-third you can look at the shape. This is subjective. I prefer a multistemmed, organic shape, raising the canopy by essentially removing the lower foliage and clutter, and revealing the tree's natural beauty in its trunks and branches. This also elevates the shrub or tree and allows the underplanting to shine. A great example of this is combination 12.

PLANTS FOR FREE

This is the best bit about having plants in your garden. Once you own them, you can create dozens, if not hundreds, of new plants from these for free. So, if you have particular favourites that you want more of, you can propagate them and fill your garden.

The easiest method for a lot of plants in this book is dividing. This is the magical process of taking one plant and turning it into many, many more. And so simple to do as well. As a rule of thumb, I would avoid trying to divide or multiply your plants in their first year. Let them settle in, find their roots, and adapt to their new home. But from year two onwards, fill your boots and exploit those plants to fill your garden without breaking the bank.

Clump-forming perennials, as the name suggests, will spread over time and grow larger. To keep them healthy, in the autumn or winter, once the plants have died back and are no longer growing, dig the plant out of the ground. A sharp spade is essential for this. Then simply chop vertically through the roots to divide the plants into chunks; I often use an old saw to do this (see opposite, bottom left). Each chunk can be about 15 x 15cm (6 x 6in), but feel free to go bigger or smaller: the smaller the chunks, the more plants you will create but the longer they will take to recover. That's it, you've generated lots of plants for free.

I don't cover other methods here, but there are entire books on when and how to propagate. My favourite is *RHS Propagating Plants*, a comprehensive guide to how to multiply your plants for free.

PLANT LIFESPANS

I have been growing plants my whole life, and no matter how much you care or look after something, sometimes it just doesn't work out as intended. Don't take it personally, it's not you. Dig out the offending specimen and compost it. Unless you can pinpoint what went wrong (and know that you can correct it), replace it with something else.

DESIGNING A COMBINATION

Designing with plants (or playing with plants as I prefer to call it) and working out what grows together is a particular passion of mine. There are no right – or wrong – ways to put plants together; anything creative is naturally subjective.

There are quite literally endless ways to combine plants. Indeed, nature has been doing it for millennia, and will always find new ways to mix plants, colours, and textures. I take inspiration from nature, from how and where a plant is growing, to colour combinations that inspire and delight.

We can assume that all plants must be planted in suitable conditions (which are detailed throughout this book and especially in the plant combination guide on pages 202–13). Given that this is the case, what makes several plants grouped together work to become more than the sum of their parts and enhance your outdoor space?

DESIGNING IN FOUR DIMENSIONS

I often refer to planning a planting combination as designing in four dimensions. With anything design related, be it art, fashion, interiors, or indeed gardens, you are always considering 2D and 3D: how the chosen subject works within the space, colours, textures, and compositions.

Planting design certainly considers these features, but there is one big difference: plants grow. This is the most exciting aspect of gardening and creating a garden. From a seed or small plant, costing very little, you can create a design that evolves and grows over time. This is the fourth dimension – time – and the plants will change through the seasons, and even week on week.

Designing with plants is like creating a painting that constantly transforms, that is never quite finished, changing day by day. While it may have its peak season of interest, the crescendo as the plants erupt into full flower, the journey to get there, and the aftermath can be just as exciting and joyous as the moment itself.

COMBINATION 22

HOW PLANTS CHANGE A SPACE

The fun bit of designing a combination is how the plants go together and, more so, how they then make you feel. Plants fundamentally change a space. Any garden I have ever created, from the RHS Chelsea Flower Show to my own front garden, is all about using the plants in a way to affect how people see and feel within a space.

The plants also affect the way in which people use the space, often for a fraction of the cost of a physical structure, and with the obvious added benefits of them being much softer and more environmentally friendly. For example, I use trees to provide shelter, but more to create the architecture and form that holds a space together. The perennials and underplanting will provide the journey and dictate how a space feels. Careful composition of colours and textures can entirely change how a space works – consider how different planting bright yellows would be compared with a garden made up of soft pastels. The use of grasses and foliage adds texture and holds a space together, while shrubs and topiary can provide punctuation, defining viewpoints and dictating journeys. Plants can be used to screen areas that are unsightly or even create a feeling of enclosure and intimacy.

What plants you use, and how you use them, can and will entirely change the feeling of an outdoor space.

FIVE FACTORS FOR CHOOSING WHAT GROWS TOGETHER

Here are the five main considerations that I use throughout this book to assemble the plant combinations.

1) COLOUR

Colour is such an important aspect of all our lives, from the shades we paint the walls in our homes, to the clothes we wear. Even subconsciously, the colours that surround us impact our thoughts and feelings. Day to day, without us realizing, advertisers use colours to influence decisions, enforce brands, and encourage sales.

The colours we use in our own outdoor space – from a tapestry of calming greens to eccentric or loud, vibrant colours – are therefore key to how the space feels, and how we use it. I have tried to offer a variety of options throughout this book to suit a number of tastes, but you can use the combinations as a starting point to dial up or down to suit your personal preferences.

2) SEASONAL INTEREST

What happens before and after the main show is just as important as the show itself. Most plants will naturally provide you with much more interest than they are credited for. Nobody talks about the way an aster first emerges, for example – how its young foliage erupts from the earth creating a verdant carpet of green throughout spring. While the main event is the flowering itself in mid- to late summer, the foliage teases you with the promise of what's to come. The post-show party is not to be underestimated either, as the flowers fade to seedheads, and the foliage crisps in the first frosts of the season. Including plants that work hard throughout the year can be as important as choosing plants that flower or peak at different times of the year.

3) TEXTURE

The foliage can be just as, if not more, important than the flowers. Without this green foil, flowers would have nothing to bloom against, nor anything to glue them together. From the elegant and erect leaf shards of a tall grass to low ground-cover foliage, from the dense clipped foliage of a topiary ball to jungle-like large-leaved plants, non-flowering plants (or those with flowers that are just a small part of their appeal) are hugely important for creating a cohesive display.

These plants soften edges while providing structure, working hard to retain their space in a garden. When spending your hard-earned money on plants for your garden where planting real estate is at a premium, it can be hard to find the restraint required to avoid a flowering plant in favour of a grass or plant that is only going to add foliage to the garden. It is so important to do it though.

Indeed, large drifts of grasses or foliage-heavy plants can be as impactful if not more so than a floriferous border. I use many grasses throughout this book and consider them a staple for creating a beautiful combination.

Colour
Keeping to a restrained palette – here, green and deep burgundy – can produce a more coherent display.

Form
Including this large specimen calycanthus adds structure to the planting. Pruning out some of the lower branches allows the underplanting to drift through.

Texture
The frothing hakonechloa grass catches the breeze, adding a different texture to the planting.

Seasonal interest
The penstemon provides additional colour in the summer months.

COMBINATION 36

Designing a Combination 23

Umbel

Globe

Spire

4) FLOWER SHAPE AND HABIT

There are eight main flower shapes, and most plants will fall into one of these groups. There are, naturally, dozens if not hundreds of variations, so this is somewhat of a generalization, but I hope it will be helpful in offering a way to easily categorize most plants.

UMBELS OR FLAT TOPS These have flat-topped flowers that are landing pads for insects looking for a nectar hit. Think of cow parsley in a spring hedgerow – an iconic umbelliferous plant. Achillea (left, top), cenolophium, and fennel are all umbels. They are a romantic, elegant addition, as their flower heads mostly sit atop wiry stems, floating above other planting.

GLOBES As the name suggests, these have ball-like flower heads that all but bounce through plantings with cheery abandon. These often look best en masse, I find, and can help to create rhythm in a border. This ball motif is repeated in many of the combinations in this book, most iconically with the roundest plant of them all, allium (left, centre).

SPIRES OR SPIKES These punch through planting with exciting spires of flowers, such as foxgloves (left, bottom). Often growing tall, they command attention. I prefer to scatter them throughout a border; too many can look like an army of soldiers stood to attention, but among other flower shapes, they punctuate a border and draw the eye.

DAISIES These are the most recognizable flower shape, the one we default to drawing if asked to draw a flower, with a circular centre and radiating petals around the perimeter. Anemones (right, top) are classic examples, and my favourite is erigeron, which I use often as it softens edges with ease and is prolific in its flowering.

TRUMPETS Think lilies, primula (right, centre) and daffodils, with open centres surrounded by petals that curve away. They are often extremely popular with pollinators as they produce an inviting access point. Trumpets are a more unusual flower shape, often harder to position, but the contrast works well against other flowers to create impact.

CUP-SHAPED FLOWERS These flowers, tulips and peonies (right, bottom) for example, have their petals curving inwards with one opening at the centre, creating a soft, delicate cupped flower shape.

FILLERS These are plants that froth and spill, often fairly transparent, enabling other plants to poke through and create a unified display. Abundant and elegant, they push their way among some of the more dominant players, helping to soften and create a cohesive border. I would consider nepeta, euphorbia (centre right, bottom), or annuals such as cosmos to be fillers. Their presence may not be striking, but they are working just as hard to make the combination shine.

CLUSTERS In these plants there are often hundreds of smaller flowers tightly packed into a bold shape. Verbena (far right, bottom), for example, can boast groups of hundreds of flowers, elevated above other planting and offering an abundance of floating clusters. These can provide a huge amount of impact from just one plant, and work hard to maintain their position within a border.

Daisy-shaped

Trumpet

Cup-shaped

Some flower shapes are easier to combine than others, but the key is to use different shapes together. For example, a classic combination is balls, clusters, and umbels, with delicate grasses to glue them together. When you analyse a planting palette you enjoy, you can often break it down into its flower shapes, and the proportions of each that have been used. This can be replicated, even with different plants. Combinations often look cluttered and messy when too many flower shapes are used. Restrained is often best, and easiest.

5) FORM

No matter how small your outdoor space, I confidently declare you can still fit in a shrub or tree. I have had various postage-stamp-sized gardens in my adult life, from a tiny balcony to an even smaller courtyard. In each, I planted a tree first. Not a huge one, and certainly in a container, but immediately it transformed the space. The area instantly feels cooler and calmer as the tree breaks up harsh concrete walls or filters intense sunlight. The structure of a shrub or tree, or even a topiarized ball, brings definition into the space.

How you use your space is entirely up to you. The points above are intended to guide you through my thought process when I consider what plants may or may not look good together. But if in doubt, plant it and see what happens. If you like it, keep it, if you don't, well you can always move it and try it in a different place alongside a different plant. Hopefully some of the combinations I have curated in this book work for you or inspire you. Have fun, enjoy the process as much as if not more than the results, and embrace the fact that it might end up looking different to how you imagined. That's the magic.

Filler

Cluster

SPRING

1

PEAK INTEREST Late spring to early summer

TIME TO PLANT Autumn or early spring

GROWING CONDITIONS This combination of plants performs best in a sunny position in well-draining soil. It will tolerate some shade, so don't worry too much if it's under the dappled shade of a tree for some of the day. Ultimately, the plants are all tough and easy to grow, so get them in the ground and let them do their thing.

INGREDIENTS

Sage Love and Wishes *Salvia* Love and Wishes PFP

Dark purple Siberian melic *Melica altissima* 'Atropurpurea'

Peony 'Sarah Bernhardt' *Paeonia lactiflora* 'Sarah Bernhardt' AGM

Simple but powerful, this combination of just three plants works extremely well to create a romantic haze of purples. Even the grass has purple flowers, so this is one for you romantics.

Everyone loves a peony, a traditional British classic that encapsulates the arrival of late spring. It's as interesting in bud as it is in flower (in fact I prefer it in bud, just as the petals begin to burst through the dark purple case). Salvia Love and Wishes is an unusually coloured variety that works brilliantly against the delicate pink of the peony. The melica is a beautiful, soft grass that helps to hold the more dominant plants together. Its delicate green foliage acts as a great foil, and then in late spring, deep purple flower spikes emerge from within its green cloak, dangling like fishing rods through and over the other plants, creating an additional spark of interest.

This is a combination that works best in clumps or drifts, scalable to the size of your outdoor space. I would recommend using a minimum of three of each plant to create the desired dramatic effect, and you can increase this proportionately to the space you have to fill.

The peonies work better towards the back of the border, as these will be the largest. They do require staking, otherwise they tend to flop over, particularly in heavy rain. I often use prunings of birch or hazel stems to help support them (see combination 9).

Scatter the melica throughout in drifts between the peonies and salvia to glue the combination together.

TOP TIP Embrace the romance of this combination and bring it into your home or gift it to a loved one. By cutting the flowering stems frequently you will encourage the plants to keep blooming and, in return, you will get a beautiful, free bouquet every few weeks.

2

PEAK INTEREST Early to mid-spring

TIME TO PLANT Early to late autumn

GROWING CONDITIONS These plants will grow best in a problematic shady corner in which nothing else seems to thrive. Keep well watered during the summer.

Trying to find plants, never mind a combination of plants, that can not only survive in a dark corner of the garden, but will actively brighten it, is a challenge for many gardeners. This combination provides an uplifting solution for those tricky spots.

The centrepiece of this early-performing combination is the structural acer, a small tree often most celebrated due to its peeling bronze bark (hence its common name of paperbark maple) and its autumnal foliage. However, for me, the moment when it first comes into leaf signals the start of spring and is just as, if not more, exciting than its famed autumnal metamorphosis (see combination 62).

The euphorbia and leucojum provide spring-flowering interest, brightening the combination and bringing it to life. They are calmed by the neutral fern species, which do such an important job of holding the combination together and allowing the flowering plants to do their thing.

Epimedium is the hidden gem here. Although it's small and delicate, the bronze-green foliage creates essential ground cover, and just peeking their way through this are its dainty flowers, which sparkle and delight. A truly great plant that is very underused in my humble opinion!

As everything revolves around the structure and form of the multistemmed acer, position this first so it can take pride of place. The dryopteris species are the constant, providing a tapestry of green structure throughout the year, and if you are covering a large area, don't be afraid to plant these in large groups. In smaller areas, allow for 60 per cent of the planting space to be ferns.

The epimedium is the smallest plant, so is best positioned at the front. Over time it will begin to scramble and cover any open ground, helping to maintain moisture. Lastly, the flowering euphorbia and leucojum can be sprinkled randomly throughout, providing you with sporadic flashes of white and yellow in mid-spring. This combination will create a lovely microclimate, with the acer shading the plants below and keeping them cool.

INGREDIENTS

Paperbark maple *Acer griseum* AGM

Mrs Robb's bonnet *Euphorbia amygdaloides* var. *robbiae* AGM, PFP

Summer snowflake 'Gravetye Giant' *Leucojum aestivum* 'Gravetye Giant' AGM

Large-flowered barrenwort *Epimedium grandiflorum*

Male fern *Dryopteris filix-mas* AGM

Copper shield fern *Dryopteris erythrosora* AGM

TOP TIP When the euphorbia plants have finished flowering, cut them back to the ground and you will be rewarded with a second flush of the golden flowers later in the season. Then leave the whole palette alone as the autumn shades of the euphorbia, acer, and dryopteris species will continue to dazzle into the autumn.

3

PEAK INTEREST Mid- to late spring

TIME TO PLANT Autumn or early spring

GROWING CONDITIONS This "Goldilocks" combination prefers not to be too sunny, and not too shady. If you can avoid the two extremes then it will be perfectly happy with anything in-between. The same applies with watering. I know it's annoying when people write "not too wet, and not too dry", but ideally it means do your best to avoid the plants drying out completely or being saturated. That being said, this is a forgiving group of plants so don't worry too much if you miss a few days' watering!

INGREDIENTS

Meadow rue 'Black Stockings'
Thalictrum 'Black Stockings' AGM

Avens 'Prinses Juliana' *Geum* 'Prinses Juliana' AGM

Snow rush *Luzula nivea*

Spurge 'Black Pearl' *Euphorbia characias* 'Black Pearl' PFP

Oranges and pinks are not often associated with spring, and certainly not mid-spring when flowering plants tend to be calming and delicate. Think of the soft pale pinks of a magnolia or the delicate greens of the woodland floor beginning to emerge. This combination of four plants defies this delicate palette with wild abandon, offering an exciting and vibrant combination ideal for colour fanatics. This mix practically screams that winter is over and the best is yet to come.

These plants are quick off the mark to spring into flower and put on a show-stopping performance. They work well growing through one another into a colourful and exciting mixture. The geum is first to burst into flower, and gets the party started with the fieriest orange flowers that will keep on going for six weeks.

The euphorbia is the dominant plant in this combination, somewhere between a large perennial and a small shrub. Its bold flower heads punch through the other plants, showing off their intriguing clusters of pearl-like flowers. Start with these as they will grow to be the largest plants and, as such, can be planted individually.

The tallest plant is the thalictrum, which delicately wafts above the others and opens to reveal vivid pink fluffy flowers. Convention would position these plants towards the back due to their height, but I prefer to have them drifting through the other plants. This creates a much more natural feeling and, importantly, avoids creating blocks of plants.

I then do the same with the geum and the luzula, the geum producing an abundance of flowers throughout the grouping, and the grass being used as a calming green that adds just enough texture and foliage to enable the flowering plants to really pop.

TOP TIP Cut this whole combination back by two-thirds as soon as it has finished flowering, and you will be rewarded with a second flush in early summer. Don't overthink it, just do it. Anytime in late spring is normally best, but if it's a particularly warm spring, you can cut back earlier.

4

PEAK INTEREST Late spring to early summer

TIME TO PLANT Any season

GROWING CONDITIONS As combinations go, this is as tough as they come. The plants thrive on a cocktail of sun and neglect. Plant in the sunniest spot you have, and they will excel in any container or when planted straight into the ground. In both cases they prefer to keep their feet dry, so give them free-draining soil and avoid the temptation to overwater.

You may be wondering why I chose this party of plants – which would be at home on an Ibiza balcony – to feature in the middle of spring. Well, for exactly that reason. It is a reminder of the warmer times to come, a summer appetizer, and the perfect addition to any sun-lover's garden. These timeless classics should not just be reserved for the peak of summer and cast aside for the remainder of the year, like Christmas decorations in the new year. I think they can be celebrated and embraced year round. To add a pop of spring colour to this combination, I have included some earlier-flowering plants that will give a taste of those longer summer evenings.

Everything centres around the feijoa, an evergreen shrub that will hold the other plants together, creating the framework for them to perform. Go as big on this as your budget allows as it will have the most impact all year round.

The thyme and erigeron work best towards the edge, softening the perimeter and blurring the boundaries. If planted in a pot, they will elegantly tumble and spill.

The iris and stipa can then be sprinkled through the remainder of the space, with the grass providing a year-round foil and the iris an explosion of rusty oranges in late spring. I have used 'Kent Pride' as my iris of choice, but by all means swap with a different colour.

This euphorbia is something of a Marmite plant, unusual in both its textures and colours. It has taken me a while to warm to this sun-loving plant, but when it's surrounded by the right companions, it can work well. Growing up to 1m (3ft) in height and width, this is chunky and needs adequate space to allow it to best perform. Its zesty yellow flowers work beautifully against its own silvery foliage as well as the foliage of the other plants.

INGREDIENTS

Pineapple guava *Feijoa sellowiana*

Mexican feather grass *Stipa tenuissima* AGM

Mexican fleabane *Erigeron karvinskianus* AGM, PFP

Iris 'Kent Pride' *Iris* 'Kent Pride'

Mediterranean spurge *Euphorbia characias* subsp. *wulfenii* PFP

Thyme 'Albiflorus' *Thymus praecox* 'Albiflorus' PFP

TOP TIP For a summer resurgence and to keep pops of colour coming throughout the season, sprinkle a packet of summer-flowering annuals (cosmos or verbena would work brilliantly) directly into the combination in late spring.

5

PEAK INTEREST Mid-spring to midsummer

TIME TO PLANT Summer to autumn

GROWING CONDITIONS If you're worried you may forget to water, this is one for you. These plants grow best in full sun, self-sufficient and resilient even for the most neglectful of gardeners. Make sure you have good drainage, especially during the winter – poor, free-draining soil is perfect. If you are worried about winter wet, simply grow these in a pot or other container so they're elevated.

INGREDIENTS

White pasqueflower *Pulsatilla vulgaris* 'Alba'

Red pasqueflower *Pulsatilla rubra*

Mexican feather grass *Stipa tenuissima* AGM

Bearded iris *Iris* 'Sable Night'

This combination evokes memories for me of waking up at 4am, worrying about whether my irises would be in flower in time for the RHS Chelsea Flower Show. Rushing down to the nursery, I was greeted by the sight of the deep blue petal tips just beginning to emerge from their outer shells, like brushes tipped in the finest dark ink and poised to start painting. I experienced a feeling of pure joy mixed with relief – bizarrely, I still feel that way every time I see an iris first break out of its bud.

Spires of these elegant bearded irises rise above the textural lower planting in this combination. There is beauty in the contrasting textures between the vertical, bold structure of the iris against the gentle pulsatilla and stipa, which waft beneath.

Pulsatilla has the most delicate, ornate flowers, and here I've used a mixture of red and white. Although the flowers are stunning, for me the seedheads are even nicer, revealing wiry duster-like heads that dance among the grasses.

Although they may look delicate and hard to grow, bearded irises are remarkably resilient and hardy. Their flowering stems can be vulnerable to a misplaced foot or curious dog, but they are much tougher than they first appear. As the buds unfurl, they produce large, almost whimsical flowers. I have used 'Sable Night' in this combination as I love their depth of colour, but there are hundreds of different varieties for you to choose from.

The irises are best bought between late summer or early autumn as this is when you can get hold of them as bare-root plants, with no soil on and cut back hard. Plant these first; they can look somewhat underwhelming to start with, but the following spring they will reward your patience with spires of majestic flowers.

The pulsatilla and stipa can be scattered throughout. Intermingling them randomly among the iris will produce the best aesthetic as they grow through one another, complementing and contrasting in equal measures.

TOP TIP Extend the season of interest beyond spring well into summer by including additional drought-tolerant and resilient plants such as verbena, agapanthus, and erigeron, all of which feature in this book through the Summer chapter (see p.76–153).

6

PEAK INTEREST Mid- to late spring

TIME TO PLANT Autumn or spring

GROWING CONDITIONS The edge of a woodland is where you would typically find these growing, so plant them in a shady spot that stays nice and moist (think dappled light and nothing too hot). Most gardening books will advise you that these plants prefer a slightly acidic soil, but as long as you're not planting into a chalky soil you should be fine. I've always grown these plants in general multipurpose compost and have never experienced any problems.

This delicate combination is perfect for calmer gardeners who prefer to avoid loud colours, opting instead for muted palettes. Beautifully balanced, the deep purples and soft greens of this composition gently welcome in spring. Although simple, the thistle-like flowers of the cirsium and delicate nodding flower heads of the geranium add just enough plum colour to make this combination stand out in a subtle way.

Enkianthus is a brilliant but underused shrub, its wiry stems elevating it above the underplanting and creating a vista through its low, open branches so that the lower-storey plants are not too shaded out. Not only does it provide fantastic form, but in mid-spring it also produces an abundance of delicate pink-white-tinged bell-shaped flowers that are loved by pollinators and gardeners alike.

The understorey foliage of the ferns emphasizes the woodland nature of this combination, but more importantly provides a natural texture that allows the flowering plants to show off. It honestly doesn't matter too much which ferns you use; these are just two of my favourites due to their versatile and easy-to-grow nature.

With the enkianthus being the star of the show, it's best to start with this. Position it somewhere that shows off its structure: this plant won't be the cheapest to buy so you don't want to tuck it away out of view. As it can grow up to 4m (13ft) tall, leave enough room for it to take on its ultimate characterful form.

Next up are the cirsium and geranium plants. These are the jewels in this combination that allow it to sing. The cirsium can grow quite tall, up to 1.5m (5ft) in the right conditions. Bear this in mind and sprinkle it through the planting space sparingly. The geranium plants only grow to 1m (3ft), and can be used as a mid-layer more liberally. The ferns can then be placed in the gaps to provide a foil.

INGREDIENTS

Hard fern *Blechnum spicant* AGM

Plume thistle 'Atropurpureum' *Cirsium rivulare* 'Atropurpureum' AGM, PFP

Redvein enkianthus *Enkianthus campanulatus* AGM

TOP TIP Prune the lower branches of the enkianthus, ideally in late winter or early spring before it flowers. This allows it to sit above the lower planting, rather than tangling with the perennials below. This turns what could be otherwise a fairly blocky, boring shrub into a characterful centrepiece.

Dusky cranesbill *Geranium phaeum* PFP

Male fern *Dryopteris filix-mas* AGM

7

PEAK INTEREST Late spring to early summer

TIME TO PLANT Autumn or early spring

GROWING CONDITIONS These tolerant plants are grateful for plenty of sun all day and good drainage, certainly not sitting in wet conditions (particularly during the winter). Their resilient nature makes them an ideal candidate for gardeners who may be a smidge forgetful when it comes to watering.

As hardworking a combination as they come, this is a real favourite of mine and one I've used in multiple gardens, including at the RHS Chelsea Flower Show. Its simplicity is matched only by its beauty, and if you're looking for just three plants to add to your garden that will put on a show with next to no intervention, these are for you.

Salvia 'Caradonna' is my favourite perennial for where I want to add splashes of purply blue into a garden. It produces an abundance of spires of rich purple that weave themselves among other perennials. Adored by bees and other pollinators, it also makes a brilliant addition to a wildlife garden.

The nepeta is a frothing, blue-flowered perennial that keeps going all summer, spilling over the edge of borders or pots, and softening wherever it grows. The deep foliage of the bronze fennel adds drama to the combination, providing a foil for the salvia and nepeta.

As there are no key structural plants here, you can have some fun and play around with how you plant them. I prefer to plant in groups or drifts, creating blocks of colour to add more drama and intensity. Depending on the size of space you have, plant in a minimum of groups of three, and scale upwards. Plant the fennel among the salvia and nepeta to allow it to froth throughout.

Keep cutting these plants back to extend their flowering performance. If left alone they will flower and fade away. However, if you cut them back after flowering, by about half, they will flower again, extending the season of interest right the way to the autumn. In good years, you can get three flushes from these plants!

TOP TIP Fennel is naturally a tall-growing perennial, up to 1.8m (6ft), and produces yellow flowers. We're not interested in any of that for this combination; instead we just want the frothy foliage. By continuously cutting these back to ground level when they start to become too big for their space, you will encourage them to just produce an abundance of smoky foliage to offset the salvia and nepeta flowers.

INGREDIENTS

Balkan clary 'Caradonna'
Salvia nemorosa 'Caradonna' AGM, PFP

Bronze fennel
Foeniculum vulgare 'Purpureum' PFP

Garden catmint 'Purrsian Blue'
Nepeta × faassenii 'Purrsian Blue'
AGM, PFP

8

PEAK INTEREST Early to late spring

TIME TO PLANT Between early and late autumn

GROWING CONDITIONS A relatively unfussy group, these enjoy a good amount of sun each day, but will tolerate a bit of shade. Keep them watered throughout the driest spells.

INGREDIENTS

Delavay osmanthus *Osmanthus delavayi* AGM

Allium 'Mount Everest' *Allium stipitatum* 'Mount Everest' AGM, PFP

Pheasant's tail grass *Anemanthele lessoniana* AGM

This combination is worth planting close to the house, thanks for the most part to the divine scent produced by the osmanthus in early spring. As the white allium flowers begin to open, they will put on a performance through to late spring rivalling the impact of any summer combination.

You will find osmanthus available in a multitude of shapes and sizes, and it can be bought as a shrub, hedge, tree, or even as topiary. It's a good sign that a plant is so readily available in an array of shapes as it means it's reliable and easy to manage. For this combination, I would recommend going for a shaggy, bushy form of the shrub. Nothing too clipped or formal. If you are struggling to come by this, you can buy the plant when it is smaller and allow it to grow naturally, pruning only when required to keep it in shape.

Build this combination around the osmanthus. The anemanthele grass should waft freely through the planting, creating the balance between the osmanthus and allium plants. Aside from working hard to hold the space, the grass will begin to take on rusty oranges as the seasons progress that will extend the interest of this combination well into the autumn.

Plant the allium bulbs in the autumn, even in early winter, with a generous scattering pushed a few centimetres into the soil to ensure the planting awakens with a bang come spring. One can never have too many spring bulbs, especially not allium: be bold and brave in the autumn, and don't skimp on these. Naturally the number you will require will depend upon the space you have to fill, but even the smallest of gardens could comfortably accommodate at least 12!

TOP TIP Consider adding a later-flowering plant such as the white wood aster (*Eurybia divaricata*) into the mix for an extension of the seasonal interest. It will work hard to complement the softness of the grass and osmanthus, with delicate sprays of white flowers that will emerge shortly after the allium begins to fade. These will continue right into the colder months.

9

PEAK INTEREST Early to mid-spring

TIME TO PLANT Autumn, to ensure the plants have time to knit together before their spring explosion

GROWING CONDITIONS This woodland composition adores a shadier spot – perhaps that corner where you're not quite sure how to bring it to life. Thriving in these usually more challenging conditions, these plants don't mind too much if it's wet or dry.

It's impossible to recreate or even attempt to mimic what nature does so effortlessly, but there is something so invigorating about seeing a woodland come to life each spring – that moment of looking up, realizing the first buds are beginning to break in the woodland canopy, and noticing the awakening woodland floor. This combination attempts to capture the essence of that feeling in a garden setting.

Although they are often the forgotten underdogs, cast aside in place of more impactful plants, the plants that appear fleetingly each spring like clockwork offer beauty in their subtle features. This woodland combination celebrates them before they step aside to let their showier neighbours take centre stage.

Hazel is a fantastic and underused plant that can cost very little but produces a brilliant shrub or small tree capable of holding a planting space together effortlessly. It will form the framework for this combination, lit up with verdant new foliage in the spring, and sporting curious mustard-yellow catkins in the late winter.

The dryopteris ferns will create a soft blanket of green, understated and yet unfurling in the spring and then holding the space for the remainder of the year. Depending upon the area you have available, plant these in drifts if you can, or as a minimum in clusters of three.

The geranium and aquilegia will provide the colour, a fleeting flash that will begin in early spring and finish by late spring. Scatter these throughout the ferns, without regard to order or groupings. The more random the better, for nature doesn't position its plants.

INGREDIENTS

Hazel *Corylus avellana*

Dusky cranesbill 'Lily Lovell' *Geranium phaeum* 'Lily Lovell' PFP

Copper shield fern *Dryopteris erythrosora* AGM

Common columbine *Aquilegia vulgaris* PFP

Alpine wood fern *Dryopteris wallichiana* AGM

TOP TIP If left untouched, hazel can grow into a large tree. In a smaller space, you can cut it back each year to the ground and it will reshoot to a manageable height. If you simply want to keep the shape and height of the tree in check, you can do this as often as required. Leave the tree to get to a decent size, then chop it back when it becomes too big. I tend to do this every three or four years to allow the plant to create thicker stems that can be reused as plant supports elsewhere.

10

PEAK INTEREST Mid- to late spring

TIME TO PLANT Autumn

GROWING CONDITIONS Naturally loving a shady, damp woodland environment, these plants are happiest under large trees or at least away from full sun, especially during the peak summer months when their foliage could scorch or burn easily.

INGREDIENTS

Plantain lily 'Devon Green' *Hosta* 'Devon Green' AGM

Giant blue hosta *Hosta sieboldiana* var. *elegans* AGM

This is a calming combination, ideal for lifting a dark corner of the garden. Dominated by hostas, this mix of plants puts on a foliage-rich display of verdant greens. Hostas are a brilliant plant for the spring, filling large areas with impressive leaves. Using a mixture of cultivars, this combination boasts a trio of leaf shapes, sizes, textures, and shades of green to add a more jungle-like feel to your outdoor space.

The geranium sprawls along the floor, with a much smaller, more intriguing leaf than the hostas, and dozens of pure white flowers that emerge from mid- to late spring. It's one of the first of the geranium plants to start flowering and brings with it a splash of purity that complements the soft green of the hostas.

As there are no structural plants to consider here, there are no right or wrong ways to position these plants. I feel they look best in clumps of three or more of each plant, depending upon the size of your garden. The giant blue hosta is, as its name suggests, the largest, so is best positioned towards the back. 'Devon Green' hosta is the smallest, so would be best closer to the front to ensure it doesn't get swamped by its more ambitious relatives.

The geranium will spread and sprawl if planted at the front of the group. Being a low-growing ground-cover plant, it is ideal for finding gaps of soil to cover with its beautiful white flowers.

As soon as the first frosts arrive the hostas shrivel to a mush-like consistency, so it's best to cut them back to ground level in early to mid-autumn and wait for new growth to erupt in spring.

Plantain lily 'Krossa Regal' *Hosta* 'Krossa Regal' AGM

Bloody cranesbill 'Album' *Geranium sanguineum* 'Album' AGM, PFP

TOP TIP Slugs are famously problematic for hostas, which can provide a tasty snack right through the year for our slimy garden friends. In damp years this can be amplified. I am lucky, and do not suffer too much from holey hostas. I attribute that to the birds, which keep the slugs in check. I do not use any chemicals and certainly don't recommend those nasty blue slug pellets. If you find yourself reaching for these, stop, and just grow something else – it's not worth it. Many slug pellets are poison, and they do not just poison the one critter responsible for munching upon your hostas, but also birds, hedgehogs, family pets, and so on. Pots and containers can be a good way of elevating your slug bait out of their reach (see Top Tip, combination 20).

11

PEAK INTEREST Early spring to early summer

TIME TO PLANT Autumn or early spring

GROWING CONDITIONS One great unifier of gardens, no matter the size, is that they all seem to have a problematic shady corner where the usual sun-loving plants sulk and wither. This combination is one for those tricky corners, thriving in damp and shade.

Primulas can have a bad rap: they are often found in every colour under the sun as bedding plants. Not only are these bright and hard to position without your garden looking garish but, even worse, they die each year.

The primulas in this combination can still be found in an array of colours, but will come back year after year – don't let the annual bedding types put you off. There is something quite magical about the jewel-like colour these primulas provide, like a bag of Skittles scattered among the woodland floor.

The aruncus is a wiry plant that will provide some low structure to what is otherwise a very ground-cover based combination. It produces really unusual and interesting flower panicles (branching clusters) that will waft above the ferns later in the season into early summer.

This combination works best as a mixed tapestry of colour and greens. As these plants are all relatively low growing, they will knit together over time to create a seamless combination that can bring the spring woodland floor to life.

For this reason, you can mix them up and play with the layout. There is no best way to plant these. I often scatter the pots across the ground and plant them where they land, creating a truly random composition and letting the plants do their own thing, just as they would in nature.

INGREDIENTS

Male fern *Dryopteris filix-mas* AGM

Vial's primrose *Primula vialii* AGM

Goat's beard 'Horatio' *Aruncus* 'Horatio'

Bee's primrose *Primula beesiana* AGM

Japanese primrose 'Alba' *Primula japonica* 'Alba'

TOP TIP While this works well as a combination on its own, it would also make ideal ground cover under a larger tree or shrub to add some spring interest. Just ensure the plants get adequate moisture, especially during the summer, as while a larger tree may provide the perfect dappled light, it can deprive these plants of essential water.

12

PEAK INTEREST Early to late spring

TIME TO PLANT Autumn or early spring

GROWING CONDITIONS These plants thrive in full sun, so are ideal for an open terrace or patio where other plants may struggle. With the phillyrea naturally growing in warm climates, it is a brilliant drought-tolerant addition to add year-round interest.

INGREDIENTS

Narrow-leaved mock privet *Phillyrea angustifolia*

Purple moor-grass *Molinia caerulea* subsp. *caerulea* 'Poul Petersen' AGM

This is a combination for the minimalists among us who find beauty in the simplicity of using less to achieve more: just two plants working in tandem to create effortless interest all year.

The phillyrea makes a brilliant evergreen shrub for smaller gardens due to its compact nature, growing to a maximum of 3m (10ft) tall. With clusters of highly scented white flowers in late spring through to early summer, being evergreen is not its only appeal.

The molinia below is equally hardworking, providing interest and structure for a good 10 months of the year. In spring, as the new foliage begins to erupt from the ground, it produces soft green spikes. Throughout the summer, it goes on to produce tall mauve flower tufts, which look like a haze of smoke. In the autumn, the whole plant takes on a soft butter yellow, before finally turning crispy and brown into the winter. Even in death, the structural foliage and faded flower spikes continue to be elegant, with the frosts catching them on cold winter mornings.

The phillyrea is naturally the dominant and structural plant here and needs to be the first to go in. Although we have used a fairly established specimen, there is nothing wrong with starting off with a smaller shrub and allowing it to grow. If you are starting smaller, remove some of the lower branches as we have here, creating a more open, multistemmed shape. I personally think this looks a lot more characterful and allows the *Molinia* some space to shine.

Underplant with the molinia, and don't be afraid to go big and bold. Even in a simple pot, no bigger than 50cm (20in) wide, I wouldn't use fewer than nine plants to create an impactful display. Leaving some deliberate gaps between some of the plants, as I have done, also enables you to clearly make out the structure and definition of the plants, and semi-mimics how they would naturally grow in the wild.

TOP TIP Although one of the main charms of this combination is its restrained simplicity, you could add colour for extra seasonal interest. A spring-flowering bulb such as 'Spring Green' tulip would bring a delicate touch of green and white early in the year. For extra impact later, try *Verbena macdougalii* 'Lavender Spires' for a punchy purple pop.

13

Layers of large, verdant foliage give this combination of woodland plants a jungle vibe. A tapestry of varying leaf shapes, sizes, and textures is punctuated with subtle blues and whites through the understorey of herbaceous perennials.

There is something so timeless and calming about greenery, and I have often been drawn to foliage-heavy gardens. During the heat of summer, being surrounded by a tapestry of greens and a variety of leaf shapes can be soothing and cooling.

PEAK INTEREST Early to late spring

TIME TO PLANT Autumn or early spring

GROWING CONDITIONS These plants love a moist and shady spot, so are perfect if you have a structure or nearby shelter that provides dappled shade, though they will also be happy with some sun during the day. This makes them perfect in pots on a balcony or terrace that is sheltered for some of the day.

Everything centres around the fatsia here, which can ultimately grow up to 4m (13ft) tall! Don't worry: I've never seen one get that big, and it would take it a long time to do so. But in anticipation of it growing larger than the other understorey plants, plant it somewhere with ample room to allow it to show off.

The tellima, blechnum, and omphalodes should be planted in groups of odd numbers (threes, fives, sevens, and so on), as this helps to create a more natural appearance. I then use the convallaria spread throughout to provide cohesion, tying together the other plants and adding that magical sparkle of white in mid-spring. Allow the foliage to knit together over time to extend the luscious effect.

Keep well watered, particularly in the hottest weather. Over time these plants will begin to produce their own microclimate, with the fatsia sheltering the lower plants, which in turn create ground cover that prevents too much water loss from the soil below.

INGREDIENTS

Aralia Green Fingers *Fatsia polycarpa* Green Fingers

Cappadocian navelwort 'Cherry Ingram' *Omphalodes cappadocica* 'Cherry Ingram' AGM

Lily of the valley *Convallaria majalis* AGM

TOP TIP This fatsia is not for everyone, with its unusual, large leaves dividing opinion, but I much prefer it to the conventional fatsia. If you're not keen, you can create a similar effect using a number of large-leaved foliage plants such as witch hazel (*Hamamelis*), redbuds (*Cercis*), or tetrapanax, depending upon your garden conditions and preference.

Tellima 'Forest Frost' *Tellima grandiflora* 'Forest Frost' PFP

Hard fern *Blechnum spicant* AGM

14

PEAK INTEREST Late spring to early summer

TIME TO PLANT Autumn or spring

GROWING CONDITIONS These plants prefer to be out of direct sunlight all day. The gentle shade of a nearby tree or building would be ideal. Growing best in a moist soil, they need plenty of water come the summer.

INGREDIENTS

Foxglove 'Sutton's Apricot'
Digitalis purpurea 'Sutton's Apricot' PFP

Marsh spurge *Euphorbia palustris* AGM, PFP

Baltic parsley *Cenolophium denudatum* AGM

Bear's breech *Acanthus mollis*

Shooting above a lacework-like tapestry of fine foliage is the soft apricot foxglove, opening its trumpet-like flowers from the bottom first. Each flower is tubular and makes a fantastic burrow in which bees can easily access pollen and nectar.

Cenolophium provides white landing-pad-like flower heads; it's one of my favourite plants for adding a soft romance to a combination. Electric euphorbia adds some zingy lime-yellow to the mix, while the acanthus is used as a calming foliage in this instance (it's a fantastic plant in its own right, and will grow its own flowers later in the summer, but I much prefer the foliage to its floral endeavours).

There really are no right or wrong ways to position these plants. As there are no key structural plants, they all work hard together to provide a woodland tapestry of low to mid-height. The foxgloves are naturally the tallest so, if you prefer some order to your border, they are best positioned toward the rear; I like the exciting unpredictability of where a spire or unexpected euphorbia may emerge, so would encourage you to be sporadic and random with your planting.

The main thing to note is that the acanthus can, and likely will, grow to be quite large in time, ultimately becoming dominant, so will require plenty of room. But don't be afraid to keep chopping it back to the ground, as it is purely the foliage we are interested in here.

TOP TIP Foxgloves are biennials. They grow leaves in one year, flower the next, and then die. If you allow the flowers to set seed, and then allow the plant to sprinkle these across your garden you will be rewarded with free seedlings popping up sporadically. All you need to do is nothing at all: my kind of plant.

15

PEAK INTEREST Late spring to early summer

TIME TO PLANT Late autumn to early spring

GROWING CONDITIONS Peonies love full sun, so plant them where they can get as much sunlight as possible. Avoid somewhere too exposed, though, as the wind can batter the flowers. On hot days, ensure they don't dry out. Peonies love a good fertile soil, so use plenty of compost when planting to enrich the ground.

INGREDIENTS

Peony 'Sarah Bernhardt' *Paeonia lactiflora* 'Sarah Bernhardt' AGM

Peony 'Coral Charm' *Paeonia* 'Coral Charm' AGM

I know what you're thinking. Surely this can't be a combination? It's just peonies! It's true, there are no trees or shrubs, no underplanting or later season interest – and very deliberately too. For me, there is something so beautiful in the simplicity of a peony, an iconic British staple cottage garden plant.

Late spring just isn't the same without a peony – it's one of the signs that spring is not just underway but gathering speed and knocking on the door of summer. The large but delicate flowers are a sure indicator that the weather is warming and the days are still getting longer.

These are two of my absolute favourite peony cultivars, and my go-to options in a garden. They work in tandem to provide a display of colour from late spring into early summer.

Go big and go bold. Use as many as you can afford, and in as much space as you have available, as these iconic plants look their best en masse. Plant each type of peony in groups of three for maximum impact. If you don't have the luxury of a large garden (neither do I), peonies also look superb, perhaps even better, in containers.

Peonies can become victims of their own success, with their large flower heads becoming too heavy for the supporting stems. After periods of rain especially, the extra weight of the water can cause the stems to buckle and snap under the pressure – and no one wants a buckled peony. To avoid this, use plant supports. These come in a variety of shapes, sizes, materials, and price points, ranging from expensive weathered metal ones through to harvested stems from quick-growing trees such as birch or hazel, which are my preferred option. Sticks and canes are a simple, reliable, and most importantly cheap way of keeping your peony flowers aloft. Simply push the end of each stick into the soil, leaving around 40cm (16in) above ground level. Create a dense framework of these for plants to weave their way through.

TOP TIP I prefer to buy and plant peonies as bare-root plants with no soil on their roots. This is a much more affordable way to buy peonies, which can otherwise be alarmingly expensive, especially if they are pot-grown and bought in flower. It also helps to save the planet, one plastic plant pot at a time.

16

PEAK INTEREST Mid-spring to early summer

TIME TO PLANT Mid-autumn to early spring

GROWING CONDITIONS These plants prefer a woodland spot that doesn't get too much sunlight and is away from summer heat in particular. However, cornus are extremely resilient, and will tolerate most environments as long as they get plenty of water during the hottest days.

Cornus is my outright favourite tree. I use it wherever I can as I think it has to be one of the hardest-working, prettiest, and most reliable trees for any garden situation. It works in gardens of all shapes and sizes as it's one of those plants that just performs, without issue or complaint.

The display begins in spring with an abundance of star-shaped, white flowers (technically they are modified leaves, known as bracts, but who really cares?), which start off small and green, emerging over a period of four weeks or longer. The flowers can hold for the same amount of time when they're fully out, meaning that their spring interest alone can last for up to 10 weeks. In autumn their leaves transform to fiery shades of orange, red, and yellow, and where the flowers once were there are strawberry-sized fruits. During the winter, the framework of branches retains its structure and form.

I have used a simple palette of ferns to underplant this tree, avoiding taking any of the spotlight away from the cornus. They form a tapestry of greens, adding interesting foliage.

Everything centres around the specimen multistemmed cornus here. Give it a position where it can be most enjoyed and, whether that is in the ground or in a container, allow it space to grow unhindered by competition. You want to be able to enjoy its shape, especially as it grows and matures. A container no smaller than 50cm (20in) wide would provide a perfect starting point.

For the underplanting, keep it simple. Clusters of dryopteris ferns provide a neutral ground cover. Try to avoid planting singly; it's better to have a few of the same plant used as a constant to provide texture and interest without it becoming too bitty.

You will notice here that you can see through the lower limbs of the cornus. This is very much deliberate, and it's achieved by removing the lower branches. For me, this shaping creates a much more striking tree that adds form and structure to a garden, enables underplanting, and prevents it from becoming a dense shrub. I find it best to do this pruning early in the tree's life, so the branches are small and less is being removed. However, you can do this at any time of year, and at any time in the tree's life.

INGREDIENTS

Chinese dogwood *Cornus kousa* var. *chinensis*

Copper shield fern 'Brilliance'
Dryopteris erythrosora 'Brilliance' AGM

Shaggy shield fern *Dryopteris cycadina* AGM

Soft shield fern *Polystichum setiferum* AGM

Spring

TOP TIP You could diversify and be more creative with the underplanting, perhaps even using one of the other groupings within this book (such as combination 18) if you'd prefer more excitement below. But for me, less is more, and the simplicity of the ferns affords the cornus the spotlight.

17

PEAK INTEREST Late spring to midsummer

TIME TO PLANT Autumn or early spring

GROWING CONDITIONS These plants love a sunny spot where they can bask in the heat of the day. Tolerant of drier conditions than most, they are also ideal for a pot or container. Avoid anywhere that may get really wet in the winter as they don't like their roots to sit in water for too long.

INGREDIENTS

Yarrow 'Moonshine' *Achillea* 'Moonshine' AGM, PFP

Wood sage 'Viola Klose' *Salvia × sylvestris* 'Viola Klose' AGM, PFP

Catmint 'Summer Magic' *Nepeta grandiflora* 'Summer Magic' AGM, PFP

I adore blue and yellow together. In my garden and home, I find it to be a colour combo I keep defaulting back to. These two primary colours are said to have the greatest contrast to each other. Perhaps this helps them to work more, but I just love the vibrancy of the yellow against the depth of the blue.

It's the achillea providing the vibrancy within this combination, with a plethora of bright yellow, floating, flat flower heads held above majestic purple salvia on wiry silvery-grey stems. The salvia are a deep purple but, set against the foliage of the achillea, they stand out even more than usual.

This nepeta is a particularly hardworking favourite too, with flowers from late spring through to late summer and beyond. It's a perfect addition to the edge of a border or container.

These perennials can all be planted casually as there is none that takes a dominant role. That being said, I prefer to plant this trio to best highlight each one, and that means grouping them in order of size. The achillea is naturally taller, so it's good to start with, followed by the salvia, and then the nepeta. Plant in groups with a minimum of three per group for the best impact. They will, over time, grow to merge with one another, which is a lovely thing indeed.

TOP TIP The more you cut the flowers, the more these plants will flower. This is a win-win situation as you can keep cutting stems to use as cut flowers in the home, or to give as gifts to friends and loved ones. Little do they know, or ever need to know, that the bouquet they have received primarily exists to encourage your garden plants to produce more flowers.

18

PEAK INTEREST Mid- to late spring

TIME TO PLANT Early autumn or spring

GROWING CONDITIONS There are two types of iris: those that love it hot and dry, and those that like it wet and damp. These are the wet-loving type, thriving in damp ground, and even more so if you have a pond, stream, or poor-draining soil. They prefer partial shade but will tolerate sun too.

INGREDIENTS

Copper shield fern *Dryopteris erythrosora* AGM

Siberian iris 'Caesar's Brother' *Iris* 'Caesar's Brother'

Soft shield fern 'Herrenhausen' *Polystichum setiferum* 'Herrenhausen'

This combination is quite a special one for me; it's funny how plants can be so personal. I chose this exact trio of plants in my RHS Chelsea Flower Show garden in 2022, which went on to win a gold medal. I used these as a calming palette just behind some seating, creating a soothing and simple space.

The deep blue petals of the iris peek tentatively from their outer casing in mid- to late spring, and unfurl to reveal a velvety flower, curious in shape and captivating in appearance. The ferns create a frothy, textural lower storey, with the bronze foliage of the dryopteris and lime green of the polystichum softening the edges of the display.

You can never have too many Siberian iris in a combination: the more you plant, the better they look – an undisputed fact. Plant as many as you can afford, and your outdoor space can accommodate. Keep them in large groupings, clustered together, so as they mature they can knit together to create a wave of velvet-blue happiness.

The dryopteris and polystichum ferns are much more of a secondary player here but their use is still important. They are a foil, a green backdrop from which the spears of iris foliage and flowers can emerge. Plant these freely and loosely among the irises.

TOP TIP Using just a few carefully chosen plants can often create much more impact than trying to squeeze a multitude of colours and textures into a space. Well, these three plants are an exemplar of this philosophy, with just three plants, two of which are ferns, working to create a simple but impactful palette. Try to avoid the temptation to add other plants. I know it can be hard, but trust me on this one.

19

PEAK INTEREST Mid- to late spring

TIME TO PLANT Autumn

GROWING CONDITIONS These plants are fairly tolerant of most conditions, but would much prefer their roots weren't wet, particularly over the winter (who can blame them?). They can tolerate an exposed site, and don't mind quite a bit of sun, making this combination a strong contender for a container or pot.

INGREDIENTS

Allium 'Mont Blanc' *Allium* 'Mont Blanc' PFP

Macedonian scabious *Knautia macedonica* PFP

Eulalia 'Gracillimus' *Miscanthus sinensis* 'Gracillimus'

Spherical flower heads of white allium stand to attention above soft grasses and romantic, crimson knautia. I love planting alliums: they provide so much joy and impact for such little cost. The impressive globes are laden with hundreds of individual flowers, adored by pollinators.

The knautia produces pincushion-like flowers, floating above delicate foliage. As the season progresses, they grow to a similar height to the allium, which by then is starting to fade, providing successional flowering from mid-spring onwards. The grasses, while soft and delicate when young, won't stay that way, soon growing much taller than both the allium and knautia.

This is a deceiving combination, one that withholds its true size and impact for later in the season. The alliums are seemingly the star of the show here, and in early to mid-spring, they certainly are the main talking point. This quickly evolves though, with the knautia and miscanthus beginning to take over into late spring and beyond.

While it may not appear that way at first, the miscanthus are in fact the most dominant plant here. In spring their emerging, verdant, soft foliage is a brilliant foil to the flowering plants, but by summer and autumn, they will be close to 1.8m (6ft) tall and forming an impressive structure. Bear this in mind when buying and planting these: you won't need too many to make a big impact.

The allium (I have used white ones here, but any would work) can be sprinkled freely. I tend to scatter these randomly around the perennials and plant them where they land for the most naturalistic and cohesive effect.

TOP TIP Knautia can succumb to a fungus called mildew quite quickly, especially in summer if the plants dry out or become stressed. This tends to happen most often once they have finished flowering and lose a bit of energy. While it isn't anything to worry about, it can be unsightly. To avoid this, in late spring once they have finished their first flush of flowers, I cut them back hard to the ground. The plants then put all their energy into new foliage and flowering again later in the season.

20

PEAK INTEREST Early to late spring

TIME TO PLANT Autumn or early spring

GROWING CONDITIONS Wet and moist! This combination thrives in those damp, boggy, and shady conditions in which most other plants would struggle and refuse to grow. Naturally these plants would be found growing by a stream or pond, but they will make the most of any area of your garden that tends to stay boggy and wet.

Now, I'm not expecting you to have a stream or pond in your garden – I don't, and I'm extremely jealous of anyone who does. Many gardens will instead have a corner where the water will naturally soak away to, that tends to sit wet for much of the year. This is the spot to plant these plants, and they will thank you for it.

This is a foliage-heavy combination, with a tapestry of large leaves dominating the space. The white from the primula is a gentle addition of colour. The hostas will also flower, but that's almost an unintended byproduct of this combination, which is otherwise all about the spring greens. Its beauty is in its simplicity.

This bold combination can work brilliantly in a pot, which also helps to make it slightly more difficult for those pesky slugs and snails to reach. Growing in a pot will also prevent some of the larger-growing plants from taking over too much. Whether it be an old pot, barrel, or other container, just make sure it gets enough water.

I have chosen a palette of large-leaved perennials to achieve a lush effect, the largest being the rheum, which dominates the space, and will ultimately grow to a few metres in height and width. Start with this, and make sure you leave plenty of space for it to grow and establish. In a smaller garden, feel free to miss it out, perhaps using another hosta or fern in its place.

While I have used different hostas to give a variety of foliage texture, you can mix this up and choose your personal favourites. The blechnum is one of my favourite ferns for its foliage, as it sends up spires of contrasting texture to the other plants. Mix up all these foliage plants randomly for the best effect; honestly, they will work in just about any order you choose.

Use the primula as the finishing touch, a delicate addition that can be planted towards the front to ensure it doesn't get swamped out by the larger leaves of the other plants.

INGREDIENTS

Japanese primrose 'Alba' *Primula japonica* 'Alba'

Rhubarb 'Atrosanguineum' *Rheum palmatum* 'Atrosanguineum'

Hard fern *Blechnum spicant* AGM

Plantain lily 'Devon Green' *Hosta* 'Devon Green' AGM

Plantain lily 'Krossa Regal' *Hosta* 'Krossa Regal' AGM

TOP TIP If you're growing this combination in a pot, and find that the slugs and snails love it as much as you do, consider installing a copper ring around the rim of the pot – literally, a strip of copper metal. You can pick these up online or in your nearest garden centre very cheaply. The copper acts as a barrier as slugs and snails dislike how it reacts with their mucus.

SUMMER

21

PEAK INTEREST Midsummer to early autumn

TIME TO PLANT Spring

GROWING CONDITIONS This combination adores full sun, good drainage, and a soil that isn't too wet, particularly during the winter. It's perfect for growing in a container, too, bringing a patio or terrace to life with electric colour.

INGREDIENTS

Yarrow 'Lilac Beauty' *Achillea millefolium* 'Lilac Beauty' PFP

Purple loosestrife 'Feuerkerze' *Lythrum salicaria* 'Feuerkerze' AGM, PFP

Lobelia 'Hadspen Purple' *Lobelia × speciosa* 'Hadspen Purple'

Sage Pink Amistad *Salvia* Pink Amistad PFP

A bold and brave combination you are sure not to miss, these plants offer striking, vivid pinks that don't just take centre stage, they take over the stage. Not a combination for the faint-hearted, this is an all-out celebration, a party of the loudest plants that just want to shine and put a smile on your face in the process.

The pink version of much-loved salvia 'Amistad' plays the most important role here, holding the planting together and ultimately becoming the main and largest perennial in the combination. The achillea, lobelia, and lythrum are all proudly pink, dazzling in the summer light, and attracting huge interest from pollinators, too.

As the salvia can grow large, up to 1.5m (5ft) tall and 60cm (2ft) wide, start with these plants and make sure they have ample room to do their thing.

The other plants can then be mixed throughout, adjusting the quantities to suit your space, whether it's a large border or a container. I would keep them about 30cm (12in) apart and drift them throughout the planting.

Leave the plants intact during autumn, and you may well get secondary flushes into mid-autumn, particularly in a mild year. During the winter the colours may fade, but they develop a new beauty as the skeletons of the flower stems crisp in the cold frosts.

TOP TIP If you want to tone down this vivid combination, it would also work well with some grasses to add more calming textures. Pennisetum or molinia would be my go-to plants to help mute the palette.

22

PEAK INTEREST Early summer to early autumn

TIME TO PLANT Spring or autumn

GROWING CONDITIONS Hydrangeas don't like to get too dry and will thank you for providing them with ample water, particularly during the summer. While these plants mostly prefer a sunnier spot, they will happily tolerate some shade without it reducing their performance.

INGREDIENTS

Hydrangea Strong Annabelle
Hydrangea arborescens STRONG ANNABELLE AGM

Lady's mantle *Alchemilla mollis* AGM

Catmint 'Six Hills Giant' *Nepeta* 'Six Hills Giant' AGM, PFP

With all three plants in proud possession of an AGM (see p.15), this timeless combination is made up of proven heroes of the flower border. They have effortless charm and offer endless displays of frothy goodness right through the summer.

The hydrangea is the star of the show, an English cottage-garden staple, but by no means exclusively for such gardens. Alchemilla provides an excellent ground cover, with frothing, buttery flowers nestled above calming foliage, while the nepeta billows on the periphery, adding a splash of colour against the soft whites and greens of the hydrangea.

For positioning, start with the hydrangea as this is undoubtedly the largest and most dominant of the plants. Growing to around 1.5m (5ft) wide, it will need adequate space to spread and perform. The alchemilla and nepeta can then be drifted around the hydrangea. I would suggest five of each plant to each hydrangea as this will provide the perfect balance.

Being so large and blowsy, hydrangea flower heads can flop and even snap when it rains due to the extra weight of the water. 'Strong Annabelle' is much more resilient, though damage can still occur.

To avoid this, use plant supports, which are readily available online or from pretty much any garden centre. If you are feeling creative and frugal, birch or hazel stems can provide a more natural support, pushed into the ground and woven into a criss-cross design (see combination 9). Position these in early spring, when the plant is still small and can grow up and through its new supports.

TOP TIP Both the nepeta and alchemilla benefit from being chopped back to ground level in early summer, once they have finished flowering, which will encourage them to produce a second wave of flowers well into the summer.

23

PEAK INTEREST Midsummer to mid-autumn

TIME TO PLANT Spring

GROWING CONDITIONS These plants will grow happily in full sun or dappled shade, so would be comfortable in most garden settings. They do like a moist soil, particularly in the summer.

INGREDIENTS

Anemone Regal Swan *Anemone* REGAL SWAN

Bobbles of soft pink flower heads bounce among the arching grasses, punctuated by graceful nodding flowers of the anemone, regal by name and by nature.

Bistorta is a fun plant, with its soft, fluffy-looking flowers produced en masse and creating a sprawling carpet-like effect across the front of a border. Anemone 'Regal Swan' has a truly stunning flower head, opening from a tight bud of pale pink to reveal a large flower atop a wiry stem. As it nods in the breeze it reveals its bright yellow centre and the curious blue reverse to the petals.

The molinia provides a calming constant to these two flowering plants. Although its main purpose here is in a supporting role, it also has multiseason interest. Vivid green tufts of foliage emerge in the early spring, paving the way for purple flower stems in summer. In autumn they come into their own as the foliage morphs into a butter yellow, then the flower spikelets fade to a russet brown.

Purple moor-grass 'Heidebraut' *Molinia caerulea* subsp. *caerulea* 'Heidebraut'

These are best planted in groupings of odd numbers to create the most natural appearance. The molinia is the largest of plants, so position it first, leaving plenty of space among each cluster. The anemone can then be drifted among the molinia. Being lower growing, the bistorta is best clustered toward the front of the border.

If you leave these standing during winter, the old flower and grass stems will provide structure right through to late winter. Alternatively, you can cut them back any time after mid-autumn, trimming them to a few centimetres above ground level and removing the old plant material.

TOP TIP These soft and elegant plants lend themselves brilliantly to the addition of some light-coloured spring bulbs to extend the season of interest. Bulbs such as 'Spring Green' tulip or the allium 'Graceful Beauty' would work brilliantly and they would start to flower just as the grasses emerge in the spring.

Red bistort 'Superba' *Bistorta officinalis* 'Superba' AGM

24

PEAK INTEREST Midsummer to early autumn

TIME TO PLANT Spring

GROWING CONDITIONS This fiery trio needs an exposed, sunny, and well-drained spot to perform at their best. A sandy soil with good drainage is ideal.

INGREDIENTS

Bronze fennel *Foeniculum vulgare* 'Purpureum' PFP

Montbretia 'Lucifer' *Crocosmia* 'Lucifer' AGM

Purple moor-grass 'Heidebraut' *Molinia caerulea* subsp. *caerulea* 'Heidebraut'

A smoky combination, these plants appear to be smouldering, with the crocosmia imitating fading embers, and the delicate foliage of the bronze fennel reminiscent of smoke wafting away. Bright yellow umbels of the fennel stand out against the dark and moody colourings of the other plants.

The purple of the fennel leaves and the molinia work together to create a tapestry of foliage that contrasts with the bright and bold flowers of the crocosmia, which produces an abundance of fire-red flowers throughout the summer.

I have planted these into old, upcycled whisky barrels, which complement the smoky colouring. You can pick up these barrels online for very little compared to the price of an equivalent-sized pot and, as they are heat treated, they last for a very long time.

The bronze fennel is the tallest of the plants in this combination, so it's best to plant it first. It can grow up to 1.8m (6ft) tall, so needs adequate space. The molinia and crocosmia are both clump-forming, spreading plants that are best planted in clusters for the most natural appearance. Group them in clusters of three or five, with about 30cm (12in) between each plant so that they can spread. The bronze fennel will intermingle, sending its feathery purple foliage up between the other plants.

TOP TIP While the bronze fennel is undeniably beautiful, it can become a bit of a thug, growing tall, and self-seeding its way around your garden. I don't mind this, and often find discovering self-seeded fennel speckled throughout a border a lovely thing. However, if you prefer your plants to behave and stay where they are planted, keep ruthlessly cutting them back to prevent them growing too large and going to seed. This will also have the benefit of making them produce fresh, new foliage to keep the display vibrant.

25

PEAK INTEREST Late summer

TIME TO PLANT Spring

GROWING CONDITIONS This dynamic double act performs best in full sun but can be tolerant of some shade during the day. Both plants like good drainage and benefit from keeping their "feet" relatively dry during the winter.

INGREDIENTS

Chinese fountain grass 'Hameln' *Pennisetum alopecuroides* 'Hameln' AGM

Japanese anemone 'Whirlwind' *Anemone × hybrida* 'Whirlwind'

This is a truly stylish combination of just two plants that work effortlessly in tandem to add elegant drama to your outdoor space. The pennisetum boasts brushstroke-like flower heads that waft in the slightest of breezes. Its dark foliage provides the perfect foil for its companion. This anemone is a plant that is often referred to as being "transparent" as the stems are so thin that they are hardly visible, allowing other plants to grow through them, and creating the illusion that the white flower heads are floating.

Since this is just two plants of a similar height, you can almost get away with planting however you wish. In larger gardens, don't be afraid to go bold with the pennisetum – it only improves with scale.

This anemone is a superb plant. It grows so effortlessly with no intervention required. If happy, it can also spread freely around your garden, as the flowers transition into fluffy seedheads that can be scattered by the wind. Personally, I love this free, beautiful plant that grows with no work required, but if the seedlings end up somewhere inappropriate, a quick yank will soon remove them.

As these two plants take some time to get into action, only really starting to fully perform by late summer, it would be a good idea to consider introducing some spring interest. The alliums 'Mont Blanc' or 'Purple Sensation' would work brilliantly.

TOP TIP Both these plants make excellent dried cut flowers for the home. As autumn descends, their colours fade, and the plants will naturally take on their skeletal form. At this point I like to cut the plants down, but don't wait too long as they will begin to decay in the garden. Bring them indoors and hang them upside down to dry out fully. The dried foliage of the grasses and stems of the anemone will then last for months indoors, and provide you with natural and beautiful decorations over the winter.

26

PEAK INTEREST Late summer to mid-autumn

TIME TO PLANT Spring

GROWING CONDITIONS Full sun and good drainage are important for this trio of heat-loving and drought-tolerant plants. Self-sufficient in the summer heat, with deep roots that go exploring for water, they make a great option for those with sandier soil and for gardens that are exposed.

INGREDIENTS

Switch grass 'Prairie Sky' *Panicum virgatum* 'Prairie Sky'

Blue eryngo *Eryngium planum* PFP

Perovskia 'Blue Spire' *Salvia* 'Blue Spire' AGM, PFP

This combination of sun-loving plants that dance in the slightest of breezes inspires thoughts of the larger prairies and rolling dunes where they would naturally grow. The muted tones of the salvia and eryngium add calming textures and colours to the garden.

Panicum 'Prairie Sky' is a beautiful and airy-looking grass but, despite its delicate appearance, it's extremely resilient and tough. The soft blue hues to its foliage help to create a calming foil for the flowers to pop against, and its dainty flower spikes drift delicately above the planting, catching the morning dew, the optimistic web of an autumnal spider, and those crisp winter frosts.

The spires of purple salvia grow into a small, woody shrub over time, adding structure to the combination, working hard to produce both an abundance of beautiful flowers, and plenty of nectar for pollinators.

Prairie plantings work best en masse, so if you have the space to plant in large swathes that would be a magical thing. I don't at home in my garden as I don't have the space, but that doesn't prevent me from planting smaller groups to imitate this look.

Where possible, plant in groups of at least three, and allow the plants to spread and dance among each other. Over time they will naturally self-seed and mingle. Let them. It's all part of their charm and what they would do naturally in the wild.

Cut back at the end of winter, after allowing the structure of the stems and faded flowers to provide shelter for garden insects as well as extra interest on those icy mornings.

TOP TIP If you are concerned about whether you can grow these plants due to the soil in your garden, simply grow them in a container instead, where you can easily control how much water they get. This avoids any potential problems with them sitting too wet over the winter, and brings a brushstroke of a larger prairie meadow to even the smallest of spaces.

27

This combination throws the spotlight upon a selection of plants that love to be restricted. In pots, they put on the most magnificent spectacle as the warm weather returns each year, perfect for even the smallest of outdoor spaces.

These are all iconic cottage-garden favourites, using a mixture of traditional classics such as sweet peas, verbena, and cosmos to create an uncompromising floral extravaganza.

PEAK INTEREST Early to late summer

TIME TO PLANT Spring

GROWING CONDITIONS This cocktail of summer-loving classics thrives in a sunny spot with good drainage, making it an ideal candidate for pots and containers.

When planting in containers, I much prefer to keep it to one plant species per pot, as I have done here. Rather than trying to plant a mixture of plants in one pot, which can be so appealing to do, this method creates a much more cohesive display.

The sweet peas and cosmos are annuals, which means they will only live for one year, but that's OK – their fleeting existence is well worth the effort. Both of these can be bought as small plants, but much of the magic lies in buying a packet of seeds for very little, and watching them germinate, grow, and flower. Follow the instructions on the seed packets.

The verbena and molinia are perennials, so they will come back year upon year. The balance of both annuals and perennials makes this a more dynamic combination in my opinion.

In the winter, once the cosmos and sweet peas have finished flowering and died back, remove the plants completely. Cut back the verbena and molinia in readiness for their triumphant return the following year.

TOP TIP Planting each pot with just one plant allows you to chop and change, moving the pots around throughout the year depending on what is looking its best. I have a small, rented garden at home, and this is how I have designed my entire garden. As flowers fade they get moved further back in the display, while other pots and plants begin to emerge. It is never the same for more than a few weeks at a time, evolving and improving throughout the year. This is a dynamic solution to even the smallest of spaces.

INGREDIENTS

Purple top *Verbena bonariensis* AGM, PFP

Purple moor-grass *Molinia caerulea*

Sweet pea 'Mrs Collier' *Lathyrus odoratus* 'Mrs Collier' AGM

Sweet pea 'Black Knight' *Lathyrus odoratus* 'Black Knight'

Cosmea 'Purity' *Cosmos bipinnatus* 'Purity' PFP

Cosmea 'Apricotta' *Cosmos bipinnatus* 'Apricotta'

Cosmea 'Rubenza' *Cosmos bipinnatus* 'Rubenza' AGM, PFP

28

PEAK INTEREST Early summer to early autumn

TIME TO PLANT Autumn or spring

GROWING CONDITIONS These three plants thrive in most conditions. They are unfussed by light levels and will comfortably tolerate everything from full sun to dappled shade. No matter where you live, the aspect your garden faces, or the light levels it receives, I am certain you will be able to grow this combination. Just ensure it receives plenty of water as these are all thirsty plants. You need to ensure they don't dry out, particularly during hot spells.

INGREDIENTS

Bowman's root *Gillenia trifoliata* AGM

Strawberry foxglove *Digitalis × mertonensis* AGM, PFP

Hydrangea Pink Annabelle *Hydrangea arborescens* Pink Annabelle

This romantic, soft, and welcoming trio of plants effortlessly introduces a creamy, strawberry palette into the garden.

Hydrangea Pink Annabelle, as the name suggests, is a pink form of its popular relative hydrangea 'Annabelle' and, in my opinion, even more exciting. Hydrangeas are making a comeback, and with the huge, delicate flowers of this variety, it's not hard to see why. Pink Annabelle offers a contemporary twist on an English cottage garden classic.

With the hydrangea unashamedly stealing the show into the later summer, the spires of the foxgloves and white frothy gillenia lead the way from early summer onwards. The gillenia is a curious plant: producing an abundance of white flowers, and growing to 1m (3ft) tall, it will grow around the hydrangea. As it finishes flowering, the petals drop to the ground like confetti, and are replaced with red seedheads that are almost as intriguing as the flowers.

Start with the hydrangea when planting out this combination as it's the biggest and most structural plant, holding the combination together. As it grows to be quite large, you will only need one or two to create a big impact. Plant the foxgloves sparingly throughout to allow their flower spikes to punch through the hydrangea. The gillenia can then be sprinkled through the front as it will scramble up and away from the hydrangea.

Hydrangeas have a reputation for being fussy and troublesome, but luckily this is nothing more than bad PR. The reality is that pruning and growing hydrangeas couldn't be easier. Leave them alone through the winter as their skeleton framework not only helps to protect next year's buds, but also has a delicate beauty, especially when the frost sparkles across the old flower head. In late winter, cut everything back down to the ground, right back. These hydrangeas, foxgloves, and gillenia all flower entirely on new growth.

TOP TIP This foxglove is a short-lived perennial, which means it is unlikely to live for more than a couple of years. When it has finished flowering, let it go to seed (literally just leave the plant alone and it will do all the hard work). The mother plant has now done her job, dispensing her seed, and leaving a legacy that will ensure years of foxgloves to come, completely free of charge.

29

PEAK INTEREST Midsummer to mid-autumn

TIME TO PLANT Autumn or spring

GROWING CONDITIONS These plants are tolerant of most conditions, but do need good levels of moisture, particularly in the summer. So, while they will tolerate full sun, the hotter the area the more you will need to water in times of peak heat. I prefer to plant in a slightly more shaded area, which takes some of the edge off the extreme heat.

INGREDIENTS

Panicled hydrangea 'Limelight' *Hydrangea paniculata* 'Limelight' AGM

Giant hyssop 'Blackadder' *Agastache* 'Blackadder' PFP

An iconic classic, hydrangea 'Limelight' has a billowing abundance that never fails to impress. It produces the most striking ice-cream cone-shaped flower heads, each smothered in hundreds of small, white flowers. In the autumn they flush to a soft pink before morphing into a russet brown, crisping as the first frost of the winter catches them by surprise.

Contrasting against this are the deep dark purples of agastache 'Blackadder', with spires of majestic flowers. Adored by bees and other pollinators, this is a strong-performing, easy-to-grow, hard-to-kill plant that works hard for its place in the border.

The hydrangeas can grow to become quite large, up to 2.5m (8ft) tall and wide. I never normally allow mine to grow so big, and they can be easily controlled with annual pruning (see below). Nevertheless, you want to allow them the room to perform unhindered. Plant at least three, because – why wouldn't you when they look this good?

The agastache will grow to 1m (3ft) tall, producing impressively large clumps. Plant these in clusters of three, five, or seven, depending on how much space you have to fill. I have been quite bold with the positioning of the agastache here, weaving the clusters throughout the hydrangeas for maximum impact.

Leave the hydrangea alone during the winter as the faded flower heads add seasonal interest. Prune in late winter or early spring, removing the previous year's flower heads back to the next available healthy buds. I prefer to wait to cut back the agastache until late winter as I like the structure of the old stems during the colder months, but if you prefer tidier flower beds, feel free to trim back to ground level anytime from late autumn onwards.

TOP TIP While I prefer the simplicity of just these two plants, you could add some extra ground-cover interest with a low salvia such as 'Blue Note', or a low-growing nepeta such as 'Little Titch'. Alternatively, add a plant such as geranium Rozanne that can scramble up into the spaces within the other plants, contributing its vivid blue flowers.

30

PEAK INTEREST Early summer to mid-autumn

TIME TO PLANT Spring

GROWING CONDITIONS These plants love a sunny spot with good drainage; don't let them get too wet during winter. Aside from that, they will tolerate most positions.

INGREDIENTS

Red-hot poker 'Tawny King' Kniphofia 'Tawny King' AGM

Pheasant's tail grass Anemanthele lessoniana AGM

Marsh spurge Euphorbia palustris AGM, PFP

Foxglove 'Firecracker' Digitalis × valinii 'Firecracker'

There are few combinations as bright and fiery as this one, positively ablaze with burnt oranges and yellows – it will certainly catch people's attention and ignite conversation. It's great for a pot or container, ideal for lighting up a balcony or terrace with a restrained palette of plants that work hard to bring colour in abundance.

The anemanthele holds the combination together, drifting throughout and creating a foil against which the perennials can spring up into flower. It's a truly special grass that matures throughout the year, starting off with green foliage that fades into burnt oranges, creating a carpet of texture and interest.

The kniphofia, euphorbia, and foxglove then bring the magic through fiery oranges and a plethora of yellows from sharp to muted, all working side by side to dazzle and delight.

Usually I recommend starting with positioning the largest plant, but in this case it's the grasses that need to be considered first. As they are so integral to the rest of the plants working, start by planting them in large drifts.

The remaining plants can then be sprinkled randomly throughout so that they can find their own way through the combination, erupting through the grasses to sparkle and add splashes of colour all summer.

This combination requires very little maintenance. Cut back the kniphofia, euphorbia, and foxglove in late winter when the decaying flowers have finally succumbed to the harsh frosts, but leave the grasses intact as they don't need cutting back.

TOP TIP Shrubs such as Cotinus coggygria 'Royal Purple', Cornus sanguinea 'Midwinter Fire', or Choisya × dewitteana 'Aztec Pearl' could be added for more structure. Their larger size holds the planting together while maintaining the styling of the existing perennials.

31

PEAK INTEREST Midsummer to early autumn

TIME TO PLANT Spring

GROWING CONDITIONS These plants love a damp soil that stays moist all year round, making them ideal for a more sheltered and moisture-retentive spot in your garden.

INGREDIENTS

Yarrow 'Terracotta' *Achillea* 'Terracotta' PFP

This is a simple but impactful combination of just two perennials, bold and bright with intense colours that complement one another well. They remind me of fruit salad chews, in those iconic yellow and pink sweet wrappers, taking me back to happy childhood memories of scoffing too many of them in the back of the car and feeling ever so slightly nauseous afterwards.

The electric orange-yellow of the achillea provides a brilliant contrast against the deep and intense purple flowers of the lythrum. The flat, plate-like flower heads of the achillea float above fine silver-grey foliage that adds a different texture to the combination.

The spires of magenta-coloured lythrum flowers flare up through the planting. Until early summer, they are just a mass of green foliage, and then, seemingly overnight, they open into the most eye-catching colour.

Both plants are adored by pollinators, making this a superb combination if you want to attract more bees and butterflies into your garden.

Wand loosestrife 'Dropmore Purple'
Lythrum virgatum 'Dropmore Purple' PFP

These two can be planted randomly to create a vibrant appearance. Don't worry about how you combine them; my only advice would be that more is more with plants this good. If you're planting up a large space, arrange them in large drifts for maximum impact.

You have two choices about cutting the plants back. You can do this when the first harsh frosts deprive them of their bright colours or, if you prefer to keep the structure of the old stems and flowers, you can leave them in position until late winter, just before they start to reshoot.

TOP TIP Growing these two plants in a pot restricts the roots and produces smaller plants so you don't need to worry about them growing to excessive sizes. Perhaps consider introducing some spring-flowering bulbs into the containers for a splash of colour while the achillea and lythrum are waking from their winter hibernation. Bulbs such as alliums or tulips would work well.

32

PEAK INTEREST Midsummer to early autumn

TIME TO PLANT Autumn or spring

GROWING CONDITIONS A brilliantly unfussy group, these plants are happy to put on a show in most situations. Avoid full shade where possible and ensure they are getting at least some summer sun, but otherwise they will grow quite happily in most soils.

INGREDIENTS

Mexican fleabane 'Lavender Lady' *Erigeron karvinskianus* 'Lavender Lady' PFP

Catmint 'Dawn to Dusk' *Nepeta grandiflora* 'Dawn to Dusk' PFP

Oriental fountain grass 'Karley Rose' *Pennisetum orientale* 'Karley Rose'

Cosmea 'Candy Stripe' *Cosmos bipinnatus* 'Candy Stripe' PFP

Soft and elegant, this pink-blushed combination is sure to delight on a summer's evening. These plants practically glow when backlit in the low light of dusk.

Loved by pollinators as much as humans, all the flowering plants have been awarded Plants for Pollinators (PFP, see p.15) by the RHS. This means that while they are adding a calming floral display to your garden, you can also feel good as you are helping the bees, butterflies, moths, and other pollinating insects. The nepeta in particular will be smothered with bees in summer as they hunt for a nectar hit.

This truly charming combination grows equally well in borders or pots, patios, or large gardens. It's a real favourite of mine that works extremely hard with minimal maintenance.

The grasses and nepeta are the two main players and will be the largest plants. Group these in generous clusters of threes, fives, or sevens, depending on how much space you have to fill.

Sprinkle the cosmos sparingly throughout the combination to provide an additional pop of colour all summer. As the erigeron is low growing, it would be best suited to the front of the combination. It will spread and sprawl along the floor if planted in the ground, or tumble freely out of pots or containers.

In late winter, cut the plants back to just above ground level. That's it. No specific or complicated pruning regime – a pair of shears or scissors is all you need. The cosmos will only live for one year, but by leaving the plants over the winter, not only will you have beautiful winter interest as the frost dances on the faded flowers, but the cosmos self-seed, so new plants will emerge the following year.

TOP TIP Cut back the nepeta and erigeron when they have finished flowering, normally just after midsummer, as this will encourage them to produce a second flush of flowers well into late summer and early autumn. Regular picking of the flowers for vases and gifts will also help to keep the plants pushing out more blooms.

33

PEAK INTEREST Early to late summer

TIME TO PLANT Spring

GROWING CONDITIONS Lovers of full sun, and tolerant of the highest summer heat, these resilient plants are perfect for a gravel garden or exposed location that gets a lot of sun. They like it dry, so don't worry about missing the occasional watering.

INGREDIENTS

Pale purple coneflower *Echinacea pallida*

Romantic, dainty, and dreamy, this naturalistic combination is perfect for bringing a softness to your garden or outdoor space.

Dancing oenothera float above the stipa grass, with their delicate small white flowers produced en masse, giving them their name 'Whirling Butterflies'. The grasses, soft and textural in appearance, just invite you to stroke your hand through them, being as soft to touch as they look.

The pale purple echinacea adds a splash of elegant drama above, with delicate petals that fold back in on themselves. It almost appears too graceful to be a real plant.

Mexican feather grass *Stipa tenuissima* AGM

As these plants would naturally self-seed, growing sporadically in the wild, there is no right or wrong way to position these. They are naturally a bit messy and untamed, which is part of their charm.

Use double the number of grasses to the number of echinacea and oenothera to create a tactile, textured appearance. Mix the plants when planting and within a few months they will naturally knit together in a cohesive way. If planting these up over a large space, you can start to plant in drifts, with up to nine plants per group, but always allowing some of the groups to bleed into each other.

The oenothera can get quite big over time, which can cause it to flop and become a bit tangled. I like to cut it back in midsummer by about half, which I find helps to create a more sturdy plant capable of withstanding its own flower power.

Cut back the oenothera and echinacea in late winter, or earlier if you prefer tidier borders. Personally I like to see the structure of the plants even after flowering as they transform from their summer beauty. While the colours may fade, their elegant structure comes to the fore. Don't cut back the stipa as it is evergreen, but brush out the old foliage in winter with a stiff brush.

Gaura 'Whirling Butterflies' *Oenothera lindheimeri* 'Whirling Butterflies' PFP

TOP TIP Spring-flowering bulbs would make a wonderful addition to this combination, bringing a dash of colour earlier in the year before the oenothera and echinacea begin to flower. The grasses will still be intact, so will provide a calming foil to bulbs such as alliums, tulips, or daffodils, whatever takes your fancy.

34

PEAK INTEREST Late summer to mid-autumn

TIME TO PLANT Spring

GROWING CONDITIONS This group loves the sun, embracing the summer heat and drier conditions. A sandy, free-draining soil is optimal to allow these plants to put on their best performance, especially in an open and exposed spot where other plants may struggle.

INGREDIENTS

Eulalia 'Ferner Osten' *Miscanthus sinensis* 'Ferner Osten' AGM

Rooper's red-hot poker *Kniphofia rooperi* AGM

Montbretia 'Lucifer' *Crocosmia* 'Lucifer' AGM

A bright and eye-catching combination, these are all award-winning summer-flowering perennials. Each is a recipient of an AGM (Award of Garden Merit, see p.15), and so is proven to be a great grower, and a fantastic option for your own garden.

Fiery popsicle-like flowers of the kniphofia push their way through the grasses and crocosmia. These are large, impressive flower heads that float through the grasses, with yellow bases through to orange tips; in just one flower they have an entire flame-mimicking colour palette.

This crocosmia is as red as a plant comes, adding a dash of pure heat to the combination. Flowering extensively, it comes into its own in midsummer and just keeps on going until it's stopped abruptly by the first hard frost of the winter.

The flowers contrast against the form of the grasses, with the beautiful miscanthus boasting its dark red, feather-duster flower heads that capture the evening light. They fade in the autumn but hold their structure throughout the winter.

Start with the miscanthus as these need the most space to put on a show. Large plants that can grow to 1.8m (6ft) tall, they are rewarding if you have the space for them to flourish. Plant them in clusters of odd numbers proportional to the space you have to fill.

The kniphofia and crocosmia can then be sprinkled throughout, again best planted in drifts or clumps and spread between the clusters of miscanthus for an intermingled appearance.

Cut back all the plants in late winter, chopping them down in one go. I have even seen people using a hedge trimmer, cutting the plants back a couple of centimetres at a time, and allowing the cut foliage to fall to the ground below, creating its own mulch that will retain moisture and suppress weeds in the next growing season.

TOP TIP As these plants don't really do a huge amount until late summer, you can plant some spring flowers as an appetizer while you wait for the main course to emerge and come into bloom. In keeping with the bold and bright theme, try a fiery combination of rust-coloured tulips such as 'Orange Princess', 'Ballerina', and 'Bastogne' for an eruption of bright colours to start the year.

35

PEAK INTEREST Early to late summer

TIME TO PLANT Spring or autumn

GROWING CONDITIONS These plants like it hot, hot, hot. They are ideal for an exposed position on a patio or terrace where they can bask in the summer heat. A resilient combination, they will be forgiving of most environments and even the most forgetful of watering regimes. The only conditions to avoid are where it could get too wet, particularly during the winter.

A calming palette of textural greens creates a foundation for eruptions of agapanthus, their flowers imitating blue fireworks, and shamelessly stealing the show. Tumbling rosemary and creeping thymes form a scented carpet, while the delicate brushstrokes of the stipa add texture to the planting. Overall, it's a frothy and dynamic contrast to the rigidity and architecture of the osmanthus and upright rosemary.

Although there is no question that this is a summer combination, with the agapanthus ensuring all eyes are firmly on them, this planting can hold its own all year, with enough evergreen structure throughout to carry it into the winter.

This is in fact the exact combination of plants I have in the small front garden of the home that I rent. I wanted to add more interest than just simply planting everything in pots. It allows me creativity and freedom throughout the year. I can move the pots and plants around to match their growth and what they are looking like season by season.

Start with the shrubs – the trailing and upright rosemaries, osmanthus, and convolvulus – as these will form the structure of the planting all year round. I use quite loose shapes, but if you prefer some formality these can be clipped into tighter shapes to control their size. The rosemaries have evergreen foliage; position these with ample room for them to grow, and allow space for the more textural and colourful plants to dance among them.

Stipa naturally self-seeds itself through other plants, so don't expect it to stay where you first planted it. That's OK – allow it to drift and move. The thymes will eventually creep and spread, creating a floriferous and scented carpet of herbal goodness.

TOP TIP By mixing the plants between being in pots and the ground, you can create a fun and contrasting display. Any of the plants here can be planted in pots or in the ground. It is the fact that you are diversifying your planting styles that creates the drama.

INGREDIENTS

Rosemary Prostrata Group *Salvia rosmarinus* Prostrata Group PFP

Mexican feather grass *Stipa tenuissima* AGM

African lily 'Lapis' *Agapanthus* 'Lapis'

Delavay osmanthus *Osmanthus delavayi* AGM

Rosemary *Salvia rosmarinus* PFP

Silverbush *Convolvulus cneorum* AGM

Thyme Coccineus Group *Thymus Coccineus* Group AGM, PFP

36

PEAK INTEREST Early summer to mid-autumn

TIME TO PLANT Autumn or spring

GROWING CONDITIONS These plants will tolerate most light levels and almost all soils, but make sure they get plenty of water during the summer.

INGREDIENTS

Sweetshrub 'Aphrodite' *Calycanthus* 'Aphrodite'

Japanese forest grass *Hakonechloa macra* AGM

Penstemon 'Pensham Plum Jerkum' *Penstemon* 'Pensham Plum Jerkum' (Pensham Series) PFP

Choosing favourite plants can be like picking a favourite child, or pet – it just isn't possible. It's a question I am often asked, and while there are hundreds if not thousands of plants that I love, calycanthus 'Aphrodite' is my undisputed favourite shrub.

It's easy to see how it takes its name from the Greek goddess of love, boasting the most impressive, bold, claret-coloured flowers that start in early summer, and keep flowering all summer long. For this combination, I have kept the surrounding plants simple, allowing the calycanthus to do the hard work.

Swathes of hakonechloa grass knit together to form a ground-cover blanket below the shrub, wafting as they catch the faintest breeze. They form a simple bright green layer during summer, and the foliage fades to calming yellows in the autumn.

Penstemon 'Pensham Plum Jerkum' offers a restrained but powerful hit of additional plum-purple to bounce off the flowers of the calycanthus, a simple addition to this combination that helps to bring the interest and eye back down to ground level.

The calycanthus is naturally the star of the show, the largest, most dominant plant in this collection. You can buy this from a small pot right through to a ready-to-go specimen shrub, depending on your budget and patience. As it's reasonably fast-growing, I wouldn't worry about going too small to start with, as it will soon catch up.

Whether planting in a border or a container, position the calycanthus first, allowing the plant plenty of space to grow and shine. The hakonechloa looks best planted en masse in front of the calycanthus, and I wouldn't plant less than nine to achieve this effect, but feel free to use more! The penstemon can then be scattered among the hakonechloa and under the calycanthus; again, the more you plant the bigger the impact.

TOP TIP To create the desired, open shape, simply remove the lower branches from the calycanthus right back to the main trunk or ground until you're happy with how it looks. This prevents the calycanthus from becoming blocky and dense over time. I prefer to create this looser shape that also celebrates the lower plants.

37

PEAK INTEREST Early summer through to early autumn

TIME TO PLANT Spring, to avoid the risk of any winter wet for the eryngium

GROWING CONDITIONS This sun-loving combination embraces hot and dry conditions, but doesn't like to be wet in the winter. If your garden is on a slope, plant at the highest point so the water runs away. If you are concerned about dampness, plant in pots.

INGREDIENTS

Purple top *Verbena bonariensis* AGM, PFP

Sea holly Big Blue *Eryngium × zabelii* Big Blue AGM

Balkan clary 'Caradonna' *Salvia nemorosa* 'Caradonna' AGM, PFP

You can tell when the garden cuts from spring into summer: the colours brighten, and the plants seem somewhat elevated and generally more vibrant. And none do it better than this trio. This combination of award-winning plants signifies the start of summer to me, erupting into flower as some of the first summer-flowering plants to break loose.

Verbena grows the tallest, towering above the others with an abundance of purple-topped flowers that become landing pads for bees and other pollinators. It's one of the easiest to grow, most resilient, and yet most beautiful perennials you can grow. The salvia is another of those easy-to-grow, but hardworking and maximum-performing plants that have a place in any garden.

The eryngium adds some magic and extra interest. Again, extremely resilient and tough as nails, it grows naturally in sand dunes and beaches, so can tolerate some of the harshest conditions. Its spiny yet iridescent flower spikes contrast with the salvia and verbena.

Start with the salvia. This is clump forming and so looks best when clustered together. Plant in groups of odd numbers (threes, fives, or sevens). The verbena and eryngium naturally grow from seed, so can be dotted throughout the salvias. The brilliant thing about self-seeding plants is you only need to buy a few to start with, and with a little patience they will begin to spread and multiply on their own, providing you with dozens of free plants year upon year.

Leave all the plants intact during the autumn and winter, allowing them time to self-seed, and observing the frost on the faded flower spikes. Then cut them all back to just above ground level in February.

TOP TIP Add in more structural planting for year-round interest. Low-growing, dwarf evergreens such as dwarf mountain pine (*Pinus mugo*) or common myrtle (*Myrtus communis*) would both provide additional form and interest while being in keeping with the aesthetic of the combination.

38

PEAK INTEREST Midsummer to late autumn

TIME TO PLANT Autumn

GROWING CONDITIONS These two plants just love full sun, making them a perfect summer combination for a spot with good drainage that's likely to get plenty of sunlight for them to bask in.

INGREDIENTS

Coneflower 'Goldsturm' *Rudbeckia fulgida* var. *sullivantii* 'Goldsturm' AGM, PFP

Eulalia 'Ferner Osten' *Miscanthus sinensis* 'Ferner Osten' AGM

It's remarkable how just two plants can be so bold and impactful. This is such a simple combination, but it produces months of interest throughout the summer.

Yellow can be a Marmite colour; personally, I love it, and think it brings joy and happiness into a garden and should be used as often as possible. Pollinators adore it as much as I do, and you will often see the rudbeckia smothered in honey bees all summer, drawn to the abundance of yellow, cone-like flowers.

The miscanthus provides a great way of balancing out the yellow, and its red feather duster-like flower heads that emerge from tall green and spiny foliage offer a beautiful contrast against the rudbeckia.

The miscanthus is the largest of the plants, growing up to 1.8m (6ft) tall. It needs ample space to be able to stretch out and grow. I prefer to plant in groups to maximize the impact.

The rudbeckia can then be drifted throughout, sprinkled among the grasses to add a splash of yellow and excitement as the buds unfurl in mid- to late summer.

As well as being a striking combination for the summer, if left alone these plants will keep going well into the autumn. From the first frosts they will begin to sparkle and then fade into wintry tones and structural stems. Just because the colours fade and the flowers fall, it doesn't mean they are finished, only starting the next phase of their life cycle. Cut back both plants in late winter just before the new growth starts to emerge. There will only be a few months each year where there is nothing to see.

TOP TIP While these plants work well together, you could also introduce some other plants or combinations from within this book to add more spring interest as they are waking up. For example, combination 17, with its yellow and blue flowers, complements these two plants perfectly.

39

PEAK INTEREST Midsummer to early autumn

TIME TO PLANT Spring or autumn

GROWING CONDITIONS Full sun or dappled shade would be ideal for this trio, each of which is tough and resilient, happy to grow anywhere (as long as it has the space to grow unhindered).

INGREDIENTS

Spiny bear's breech *Acanthus spinosus*

Japanese anemone 'Andrea Atkinson' *Anemone × hybrida* 'Andrea Atkinson'

Chinese fountain grass 'Hameln' *Pennisetum alopecuroides* 'Hameln' AGM

In this architectural combination, the striking spires of the unusual-looking and dominant acanthus are softened by the simple flowers of the anemone and the textural foliage of the pennisetum grass. A palette of whites and greens, this offers calming foliage that ensures interest not just when the flowers emerge, but for most of the year.

The acanthus is a curious plant, with large, glossy, and spiny foliage that alone would make it interesting to add to a garden. However, in midsummer it adds an extra layer of excitement as it thrusts majestic spires of purple and white flowers into the air. These stay aloft all the way into autumn, like skyscrapers above a forest of green.

Pennisetum is a special grass that I love to use as it glues other plants together, providing a calming balance and softener for them to shine against. It reserves itself for the autumn when it puts on its own show.

I have mixed these plants together to provide balance, and I think each plays off the others well to bounce between the flower and foliage interest they each bring.

All of the plants here can grow to be quite large, particularly for perennials. It is key to leave plenty of space for these to grow and flourish – about 60cm (24in) between them.

The acanthus are the central plants, being the largest and most structural, growing up to 1.5m (5ft) tall. Plant them as standalone specimens; don't feel the need to group them unless you have a particularly large space to fill. The pennisetum are next up, and best planted in clumps of three to allow them to add the most impact. Finally, sprinkle the anemone throughout for pops of the white flowers from midsummer onwards.

TOP TIP While this is a brilliant group for summer, these plants will also become a beautiful autumnal composition if left alone and allowed to transform into their seasonal attire. The grasses will take on yellow hues, and the flower heads of the acanthus and anemone will fade while maintaining their structural appearance, adding to the architectural qualities of this combination.

PEAK INTEREST Midsummer to mid-autumn

TIME TO PLANT Early to mid-autumn or spring

GROWING CONDITIONS These plants thrive in full sun with good drainage. They are ideal for a sandier soil that doesn't stay too wet during the winter.

INGREDIENTS

Eulalia 'Gracillimus' *Miscanthus sinensis* 'Gracillimus'

Culver's root 'Fascination' *Veronicastrum virginicum* 'Fascination' PFP

A combination of just two plants, this hardworking duo is perfect for adding simple elegance to the back of a border where you require height and form, but don't want anything as structural as a shrub or tree.

These plants can grow tall, with the veronicastrum reaching 1.5m (5ft) and the miscanthus even taller at 1.8m (6ft). They may not work so well for a smaller patio or terrace, but are ideal for a larger space that needs filling, where simplicity and restraint is desired. The veronicastrum is a curious plant, with simple violet spires that punch through the grasses like arrows pointing skywards. It's softened by the spreading form of the miscanthus, which produces an abundance of verdant foliage from spring through to summer then, in mid- to late summer, begins to bloom with plumes of feather duster-like flower heads.

There isn't really a right or wrong way to group these plants together. Normally I would advise planting in clusters, proportional to the size of the garden or space you are looking to fill, but I think this duo works best intermingling and growing through each other. So throw away the rule book and plant however you like – they'll work it out and look good regardless, so long as they have the space and height to do what they do best.

Leave well alone into autumn and winter as, although they may finish flowering during the summer, their autumnal attire matures beautifully, with the miscanthus foliage taking on butter yellows and their flower heads holding strong into the winter. As the frost and ice of a cold winter's day illuminate the now crispy stems of both plants, they transform into almost entirely different plants from their summer displays.

Cut both plants right back to the ground in late winter before they start to reshoot, and then leave well alone for the following 12 months: they will do the hard work themselves.

TOP TIP Add these plants to other combinations within this book, such as 29 or 44, to bring lower plants into the foreground, and let these back of the border beauties create a backdrop and boundary.

41

PEAK INTEREST Early to late summer

TIME TO PLANT Spring or autumn

GROWING CONDITIONS Plant somewhere that will receive full sun, but not too exposed. Strong winds can damage the soft new growth of the salvia, while messing up the tufted, hairlike appearance of the grass. These plants are drought resilient, so can tolerate extreme heat, but make sure the soil can drain freely in the winter so they don't sit in the wet.

INGREDIENTS

Tufted hair grass *Deschampsia cespitosa*

A fine balance between grasses and flowers, simple but striking, this combination would work well in any garden environment: traditional, contemporary, minimalist, or cottage style. If you're looking for a quick and easy way to improve any garden area, large or small, these two plants won't let you down.

Salvia 'Amistad' is one of my all-time favourite garden plants, with velvety purple trumpet-shaped flowers attached to striking black stems that emerge from verdant, fresh foliage. It is normally smothered in flowers that just keep going all summer.

Deschampsia is a grass I just love to use. I have included it not only in every show garden I have designed, but also in every domestic garden. It is simple, easy to grow, and hardworking. Each summer it sends out a profusion of flower spikes, creating a balance between being dense and transparent, contrasting here against the salvia, but also working well with just about any perennial.

Sage 'Amistad' *Salvia* 'Amistad' AGM, PFP

Both these plants will ultimately grow to around 1m (3ft), making them ideal for planting direct in the ground or in a container. Wherever you choose, make sure you allow space for them to grow and spread out.

Planting in groups of three or more produces the best impact. I like to merge the groups, with the odd grass outriding into a cluster of the salvia for a more mixed and softened aesthetic, just as in the example I have created.

TOP TIP While these two plants are some of the first of the summer flowers to get going, there aren't going to be many blooms before then. Some spring-flowering bulbs in muted colours, such as the tulips 'Spring Green' or 'Queen of Night', allium 'Mont Blanc', or narcissus 'Thalia', would make great additions, bringing some early colour. Plant the bulbs in the autumn, scattered freely among the deschampsia and salvia, so they pop up randomly. And always remember when planting bulbs of any kind, more is more, and nobody ever regretted buying an extra packet of bulbs.

42

PEAK INTEREST Mid- to late summer

TIME TO PLANT Autumn or spring

GROWING CONDITIONS Position in a sunny spot with good drainage. Echinacea in particular doesn't like to have wet feet, so is best planted in a container if you're concerned at how damp your garden can get during the winter.

INGREDIENTS

Culver's root 'Album' *Veronicastrum virginicum* 'Album' AGM, PFP

Spires of white punch their way through soft, billowing grasses, punctuated with dustings of large coneflowers. This is a sizeable-growing trio that can hold its own in a big garden, with the veronicastrum growing up to 1.5m (5ft) tall, standing to attention with no need for additional support.

This all-white combination is sure to add a calming and soothing area to your garden. White is often hard to position, but works really well if you can strike the balance between white and the verdant green backing it needs to really stand out. The reflexed petals of the echinacea are a strong shape and they complement the spires of the veronicastrum and the softness of the pennisetum. As summer progresses, the pennisetum will produce fluffy bunny-tail flower heads that glisten in the early morning dew.

Coneflower 'Alba' *Echinacea purpurea* 'Alba' PFP

Each of these plants is clump forming, naturally growing into a larger clump each year. They are best positioned in groups of three, five, or seven, depending upon the space you have to fill. The echinacea work well sprinkled throughout so they can pop up among the grasses and create a great understorey to the veronicastrum.

Leave all three plants intact during the winter. They provide beauty in decay, offering a fantastic winter habitat for insects and a great source of food from their old seedheads. Cut them back to the ground in late winter, just before the new growth starts to emerge in early spring.

TOP TIP Veronicastrum can become leggy, often only sending up a couple of tall flower spikes in its first year, putting all its energy into these. In late spring or early summer, just as the foliage is getting going and approaching around 50cm (20in) tall, cut the plant back by half. This may seem ruthless but by doing so you encourage the plant to produce dozens more flower stems and, in turn, a much more impressive display.

Chinese fountain grass *Pennisetum alopecuroides*

43

PEAK INTEREST Early summer to early autumn

TIME TO PLANT Spring

GROWING CONDITIONS These plants like good drainage and conditions that don't get too cold and wet, particularly in the winter. If in doubt, plant in a container for better drainage during those grim winter months.

INGREDIENTS

Salvia 'Amistad' *Salvia* 'Amistad' AGM, PFP

Milky bellflower 'Prichard's Variety' *Campanula lactiflora* 'Prichard's Variety AGM, PFP

This dynamic duo of hardworking, easy-to-grow, and top-performing perennials will be sure to put on a show from early summer right the way through to early autumn and beyond.

There are few plants as floriferous as the salvia 'Amistad', with deep, rich, dark purple flowers in upright clusters that shoot up above its light green foliage.

The campanula is a much softer plant, with calmer, light violet-coloured flowers that complement and contrast with the salvia. Both are individually strong and beautiful plants, but combined they create magic.

This combination can become rather large, with the salvia reaching up to 1.5m (5ft) tall, and the campanula up to 1m (3ft); when planting, make sure to give them plenty of space to grow and stretch out. The salvia is the larger and more dominant of the two, so position them first. When you first plant them they will be deceptively small, but in no time – a matter of weeks – they will begin to fill the space. Arrange them in drifts of odd numbers.

Do the same with the campanula, which can be used more in the foreground, or mixed throughout. These big and blowsy plants make superb border fillers where you need some big-hitting, colourful plants to plug a gap.

I suggest planting in spring to avoid their roots rotting in the wet of the first winter before they have had a chance to grow and establish. When buying either of these plants they can arrive with just a few stems. This is the moment to be bold and brave: cut back what growth they have as this will encourage the plants to bush out, producing many more flowers during the summer.

TOP TIP The more you cut, the better these plants will perform, so don't be afraid to get out there with your kitchen scissors and take cut flowers for the kitchen or as gifts for friends. By continuously cutting flowers you will encourage the plants to produce more and more flower buds.

44

PEAK INTEREST Early to late summer

TIME TO PLANT Spring

GROWING CONDITIONS Reward these plants with a sunny and free-draining position, and they will reward you with an endless abundance of mauve flowers throughout the summer. They don't like to sit in wet, so avoid positions where they may get too damp: a sandy and exposed soil would be ideal. If you are at all concerned, grow them in pots as I have done here.

INGREDIENTS

Balkan clary 'Caradonna' *Salvia nemorosa* 'Caradonna' AGM, PFP

I simply adore these three plants. From their colours and textures to their flower shapes and performance, these are three hardworking plants that look amazing in just about any garden. Versatile and reliable, they flower from early summer right through to the first frosts. If I am ever deliberating what to add to a garden, these would be high on my list of go-to plants.

English lavender is a staple in any traditional cottage-garden planting. Iconic, and for good reason, its highly scented flowers are abundant. It's fully hardy and one of the most bullet-proof lavenders you can plant.

Salvia 'Caradonna' and agastache 'Blue Fortune' are purple-flowering perennials that provide as much interest for us as they do for bees and other pollinators: you will often find them smothered in honey bees looking for their latest nectar hit.

English lavender *Lavandula angustifolia* PFP

I love to plant these in clusters of three or more. This allows each clump to have its own definition and best showcases the beauty of each plant. I would do the same if planting into pots, keeping each type of plant in a separate pot for maximum impact.

Just before midsummer they should have finished their first wave of flowering. If you cut them back by approximately half, removing all the old flower spikes, they will produce a second flush of flowers in late summer and on into the autumn.

The salvia and agastache can both be cut back to ground level during winter. The lavender is best pruned at the end of summer when it has finished flowering, to just 22cm (9in) above ground level to encourage the best results for the following year.

TOP TIP I prefer to plant these in spring, once the ground has started to warm up. While you can plant in the autumn and they will likely be OK, by planting in spring you avoid any risk of the lavender sitting in the wet during the winter, which is the main reason the plant may fail.

Giant hyssop *Agastache* 'Blue Fortune' AGM, PFP

45

PEAK INTEREST Early summer to early autumn

TIME TO PLANT Spring or autumn

GROWING CONDITIONS Lovers of plenty of sunshine, and tolerant of exposed, open sites where others may struggle, these resilient plants are ideal for larger areas that are open to the elements. A sandy soil is ideal but not essential; the main thing is to ensure good drainage in winter.

INGREDIENTS

Like giant red sparklers, the miscanthus flower spikes drift above the piercingly bright orangey-red flowers of the helenium. This dazzling display is made up of just two plants that work together to create an impressive and colourful show.

Helenium is a perennial that signifies the start of summer with its exciting, vivid colours. While it looks its best in large swathes, it can be just as effective in smaller gardens, pots, and containers, brightening any garden space.

Miscanthus 'Red Chief' is a large grass, reaching up to 1.5m (5ft) tall, making its foliage an impressive statement in any garden. However, come midsummer, the foliage takes a back seat as explosions of soft red flower panicles erupt and steal the show. These are then held aloft, catching attention in the autumn as they fade and crisp up, providing structure and interest well into the winter.

Sneezeweed 'Moerheim Beauty' *Helenium* 'Moerheim Beauty' AGM, PFP

There's a real beauty in the simplicity of just using two plants. Not only do they work well together, but also there is no wrong way to plant them. As long as you plant them the right way (greenside up), they will look good and provide months of interest and excitement.

I prefer to group them into clusters, but equally they will work fine mixed up, allowing the plants to grow through each other and create a coherent display. In larger gardens, when planting en masse, drifts work better. Go big and brave, and allow them to dominate a space.

Leave them alone during the winter and cut them back to ground level in late winter just before the new growth emerges.

TOP TIP Mix in some spring bulbs to start the season of interest earlier. In keeping with the fierce oranges and reds of the miscanthus and helenium, tulips such as 'Ballerina', 'Mascara', 'Bronze Charm', and 'Disaronno' would all make great additions. These are best planted in late autumn once the cold weather commences. Scatter generous handfuls on the soil, and plant where they land to create a truly sporadic and natural appearance.

Eulalia 'Red Chief' *Miscanthus sinensis* 'Red Chief'

46

PEAK INTEREST Early summer to early autumn

TIME TO PLANT Autumn or spring

GROWING CONDITIONS This pair grows happily in full sun or partial shade. I prefer to plant them where they will get either the morning or the evening light (east- or west-facing), as the glow of the low light at dawn or dusk brings these plants to life. A free-draining sandy soil is best, but keep them watered in the summer.

INGREDIENTS

Burnet 'Blackthorn' *Sanguisorba* 'Blackthorn'

Purple moor-grass *Molinia caerulea*

Sometimes all you need is two utterly gorgeous plants that work in harmony to create a beautiful area. This can be on a small patio where you don't have the luxury of space to cram in too many different plants or, like me, you may love the simplicity of making a feature of two plants on a larger scale to create restrained drifts.

Sanguisorba is one of my all-time favourite perennials. I use it in as many gardens as I can, as it offers height and impact without being too blocky. The wiry stems holding aloft delicate flowers allow the luxury of introducing lower-growing plants in front, or of drifting these through larger planting areas.

The flowers of the sanguisorba appear to be luminous in only the faintest summer light, coming alive when backlit, almost as if they've been plugged in and turned on. At around 1.5m (5ft) tall, they are held above the molinia, poking their soft and fruity-coloured flowers through the grass stems.

Whether in containers or an open bed, I much prefer to plant these in groups. A minimum of three of each plant is required even for the smallest of spaces, scaling up accordingly for larger gardens.

They will fade during the autumn: the colours in the flowers first transform to cosy shades of autumnal russets and browns, before they lose their colour completely, leaving behind only the structure of the old stems and dried flower heads. You don't need to do anything for several months, but in late winter, just before they begin to reawaken, cut the old growth back to ground level, and let the whole process repeat.

TOP TIP I'm sharing some of my other favourite sanguisorba varieties here. 'Tanna' makes a fantastic low-growing option for smaller gardens, reaching only 50cm (20in). 'Cangshan Cranberry', on the other hand, is one of the tallest available, growing to an impressive 2m (6½ft). *Sanguisorba menziesii* is one of the first to flower, normally starting in late spring and continuing through the summer. If you can, I recommend planting at least one type of sanguisorba in your garden.

AUTUMN

47

PEAK INTEREST Late autumn

TIME TO PLANT Autumn or spring

GROWING CONDITIONS This combination loves drier conditions, preferably a spot that gets drenched in summer sun. Don't let them sit in the wet during the winter, and if necessary plant them in a container.

INGREDIENTS

Pheasant's tail grass *Anemanthele lessoniana* AGM

Winged spindle *Euonymus alatus*

This euonymus is one of the most striking plants you can grow, and is sure to light up your whole neighbourhood, never mind just your garden, with its electric colours. Its Day-Glo pink foliage in autumn is joyful and not overpowering, bringing excitement into the garden just before the winter cold sets in. Alongside its fluorescent foliage there are small, orange, jewel-like berries that add to the colour. During the winter, as its leaves fall and expose its naked branches, one last curiosity is revealed: the stems are winged, with ridges of bark running along each branch.

It is underplanted with one of my favourite steadfast grasses, anemanthele, the pheasant's tail grass, which only gets better as the year progresses. As it catches a slight breeze its arching flower stems dance, creating a soft, billowing effect. In the autumn the foliage morphs to rusty oranges, and it carries these russety tones through the winter.

Everything centres around the majesty of the euonymus, which could be considered a large shrub rather than a small tree. Position this as you would a sculpture, where it can be shown off and add structure to your space. If you are planting in a container, this lifts the whole combination so you can see the beautiful internal structure of the euonymus.

The grasses are underplanted around it to create a carpet, softening the edges and adding texture and interest below. That's it: simple and restrained, but bold.

TOP TIP While the main season for the euonymus is autumn, the rest of the year it has green foliage, waiting patiently for its time to change and dazzle. You may wish to bring brighter colouring into the combination earlier, planting bulbs such as the tulip 'Ballerina' or allium 'Red Mohican' to form a contrast against the softness of the plants earlier in the season.

48

PEAK INTEREST All year round

TIME TO PLANT Spring or autumn

GROWING CONDITIONS Choose somewhere in full sun, exposed, and with good drainage. These plants thrive in the summer heat – the hotter the better – bringing a splash of the Mediterranean to your garden.

INGREDIENTS

Narrow-leaved mock privet *Phillyrea angustifolia*

Silver spear *Astelia chathamica* AGM

Mexican feather grass *Stipa tenuissima* AGM

In a time of more extreme weather conditions, these three are the definition of resilient: remarkably tough and easy to grow.

Phillyrea is a superb plant for adding structure. It is a lesser-used alternative to yew, buxus, or ilex, all of which are more commonly found as topiary balls. Phillyrea is much tougher than these, with its waxy silvery-green foliage that responds brilliantly to being clipped. It is underplanted with astelia to continue the silver effect, with its spears of sharp-looking foliage, and balanced with the delicate and fluffy stipa.

Start with the phillyrea. I have used plants already clipped into topiary balls, but you can buy these as smaller shrubs and clip them into a ball yourself. It's simple to do, but I'm a bit impatient and prefer to see them look good straightaway.

The astelia are the next most structural plant, in time becoming dominant within the space, and architectural in their own right. Their steel-coloured foliage erupts through the softness of the stipa, so you don't need too many to create a substantial impact. The stipa works best in drifts, mingling among the other plants to soften what could otherwise be a rather dominant scheme.

All the plants are evergreen, so will provide interest right through the winter. Basically leave them alone; the only maintenance that might be required is to occasionally trim the phillyrea, and use a comb to remove the old growth from the stipa once a year.

TOP TIP The temptation with any topiary can be to clip it often to keep it defined, but with phillyrea I prefer to see the shaggier growth when it is unclipped. They lend themselves to being looser in shape, looking softer, fluffier, and more natural. I try to trim it no more than twice a year and cut it back well when I do.

49

PEAK INTEREST Spring and autumn

TIME TO PLANT Spring or autumn

GROWING CONDITIONS These plants prefer a dappled corner, somewhere sheltered from full sun in the peak of summer, and away from extreme winds. They are ideal for a shadier nook that offers some protection.

INGREDIENTS

Flowering dogwood red-form *Cornus florida* f. *rubra*

Ivy-leaved cyclamen *Cyclamen hederifolium* AGM

White-flowered ivy-leaved cyclamen *Cyclamen hederifolium* var. *hederifolium* f. *albiflorum* AGM

Palm sedge *Carex muskingumensis*

It's all about the cornus for this display. A beautiful small tree that can add instant structure and character to a garden, with multiseason interest, this is one of my all-time favourite trees. In spring it provides an abundance of white "flowers" (actually bracts, which are modified leaves that look like flowers) that arrive in late spring and can last for as long as a month. In the autumn it transforms again. Their foliage turns ruby red, and dazzling bright red berries take the place of the spring flowers. The autumnal change of outfit is striking, ensuring that, as the winter months approach, there is one last explosion of interest.

The frothy understorey comprises a mixture of carex and cyclamen. These two cyclamen flower in the autumn, and I have mixed pinks and whites here with reckless abandon, adding a splash of colour at a time of year when most plants are starting to wind back. The carex acts purely as a foil of green, with its semi-evergreen foliage providing a cushioning base to allow the cornus to shine.

As everything centres around the cornus, I would recommend buying as big as you can afford. While you will be able to pick up small and relatively cheap options, for not a huge amount more you can buy a large shrub or small tree-sized specimen that will add instant form and character.

The cyclamen and carex can then be underplanted. I prefer to plant both in drifts, creating a textured carpet of calming tones. Use two-thirds carex to one-third cyclamen, as the flowering time of the cyclamen is only fleeting, and position the cyclamen near the front.

TOP TIP I have used cyclamen here as they provide a dash of autumnal excitement, but feel free to swap these out or include other seasonal planting. Spring-flowering bulbs such as the daffodils 'Thalia' or 'Pheasant's Eye' would make joyful additions to welcome in the new year. In summer, plants such as erigeron would soften the understorey. Feel free to get creative and plant what you enjoy.

50

PEAK INTEREST Late summer to autumn

TIME TO PLANT Spring

GROWING CONDITIONS This trio adores the hotter weather, embracing dry and sunny conditions most plants would struggle to grow in, never mind thrive. They can also be surprisingly tolerant of winter cold, but they do not like winter wet, so it's better to grow them in containers if your soil stays wet in the summer.

INGREDIENTS

Strawberry tree *Arbutus unedo* PFP

Tufted hair grass *Deschampsia cespitosa*

Switch grass 'Rehbraun' *Panicum virgatum* 'Rehbraun'

This is a combination you may expect to see in Italy, while dining alfresco on a late summer evening, sheltering under the dappled shade of the arbutus as the grasses drift effortlessly underneath. Known also as the strawberry tree, the arbutus produces miniature Christmas bauble-like fruits, no bigger than a small tomato, which look almost artificial, especially on a frosty morning when coated in ice. They evolve through bright shades of yellow, orange, and red, often with each cluster of fruits displaying a variation of all the colours at once. It flowers and fruits at the same time, with clusters of white bell-shaped flowers alongside the fruits from the previous year's flowers.

The two grasses are very much the backing vocalists here, a supporting role to uplift the arbutus, but they do provide much-needed lower-storey texture and movement. With year-round interest from their juvenile fresh green foliage in the spring, through to the skeletons of the old flower heads and foliage in the winter, they provide a pulse and rhythm.

The arbutus is our primary focus here. It's naturally a sculptural, architectural tree, ideal for adding form and interest, or even as screening with its evergreen foliage, but in a much more pleasing way than a simple hedge. Position the tree where it can be of most value, allowing it space to grow and shine.

The two grasses are then used for underplanting. Arrange them in drifts under and around the arbutus, in groups of three, five, or seven, depending on the space you have to fill.

TOP TIP The bark on the arbutus is stunning. It peels away to produce a snakeskin-like textured effect, improving with age. I like to remove lower branches, exposing the bark so it isn't hidden under the foliage. Taking off the lower stems right back to the main trunk opens up the framework of the tree.

51

PEAK INTEREST Late summer to autumn

TIME TO PLANT Spring

GROWING CONDITIONS Lovers of full sun, these plants not only tolerate drier spells, but embrace and thrive in them.

INGREDIENTS

Coneflower 'Herbstsonne' *Rudbeckia laciniata* 'Herbstsonne' AGM, PFP

Eulalia 'Ferner Osten' *Miscanthus sinensis* 'Ferner Osten' AGM

These two plants work together, hand in hand, to make a striking and majestic combination. Giant in size, this is a duo you are unlikely to miss as they tower above other garden plants, offering simple, bold appeal.

Despite this impressive stature for perennial planting, the effect is curiously delicate, the feather duster-like flowers of the miscanthus contrasting beautifully against the zingy yellow flowers of the rudbeckia.

When positioning, do consider the ultimate height of this combination. They reach up to 2.5m (8ft) tall, so they must be allowed adequate space to mature. Start with the miscanthus, the wider of the two plants, which will bulk out into a thicket of stiff stems that support the arching flower heads. The rudbeckia looks best woven sparingly through the miscanthus so, as it emerges, the bright yellow flowers are nestled within the grass. This will also help to act as a natural plant support, the miscanthus helping the rudbeckia to stay upright.

Leave the plants alone during the winter to benefit wildlife and insects, which will feast and live within the decaying foliage – a valuable habitat for so many essential garden-friendly insects. In late winter, just before they start to reshoot for the new seasons ahead, cut the plants back to ground level to allow them to do it all over again.

TOP TIP Plant at the back of a border where they can grow to their full potential, creating an elegant backdrop to other planting (combination 57 would pair well in front of this). Use their height to bring scale and structure that can usually only be achieved through adding in a hedge or large shrubs.

52

PEAK INTEREST Autumn

TIME TO PLANT Spring or autumn

GROWING CONDITIONS Best planted in full sun or partial shade, these plants don't mind being a bit exposed to the elements. Resilient and tough, they can tolerate drier conditions than most, but prefer good drainage.

INGREDIENTS

Seven son flower tree *Heptacodium miconioides* AGM

Michaelmas daisy 'White Ladies' *Symphyotrichum novi-belgii* 'White Ladies'

Switch grass 'Rehbraun' *Panicum virgatum* 'Rehbraun'

Heptacodium is one of those trees that no one really knows or plants, yet every garden deserves one. It is easy to grow, unfussy about its location, and will reward you with flowers and interest at a time of year when most other trees and plants are beginning to go past their best. Its flowers are both plentiful and beautiful – pure white clusters that form in early autumn, then fade away to leave only the outer part of the flower, which is the most exciting soft red-purple.

Here I have chosen a multistemmed specimen as its open form allows me to plant below with even more autumnal interest. A combination of daisies and panicum grass are used to create a soft and textural lower storey, complementing the peeling bark of the heptacodium while bringing a romantic addition to the ground floor.

The heptacodium comes first. Not only is it the largest and most dominant, but its structure holds everything together – consider it a living sculpture. Position it where it will add the most visual value; its shape and form are key for bringing living architecture into even the smallest of spaces.

The grasses and daisies can then be drifted around the base. Plant them in clumps of three, five, or seven, depending on the space you need to fill, and mix them up as you wish.

TOP TIP If you can, buy your heptacodium in person. Trees are amazing, and each one is slightly different in age, size, structure, form, or maturity, so it's worth spending a little extra time to choose one that works well within your space. I chose mine here based on its open, multistemmed shape, but you will find an array of options available to you.

53

PEAK INTEREST Mid- to late autumn

TIME TO PLANT Spring

GROWING CONDITIONS Happy to grow in dappled shade or full sun, these plants are reasonably unfussy about where you put them, but try to avoid any extremes.

INGREDIENTS

Fountain grass 'Rubrum' *Pennisetum advena* 'Rubrum' AGM

Oak-leaved hydrangea *Hydrangea quercifolia*

Chinese fountain grass 'Hameln' *Pennisetum alopecuroides* 'Hameln' AGM

Autumn is a time for pumpkin soups, spiced lattes, frolicking in leaves, and crisp walks. It's also the season of deep maroons, russets, and striking crimsons, a period where colours become deeper, richer, more exaggerated, and bolder. One of the reasons I love autumn so much is the evolution of a tree or planting from verdant greens to its autumnal attire, entirely changing the atmosphere, like one last explosion of colour before the winter cold sets in.

The plants in this combination manage to bottle this feeling, condensing the colours and textures of autumn into a collection that feels warm and charming. The large oak-leaf-shaped foliage of the hydrangea takes on a deep, rich claret, striking from a distance and even better close up.

These large leaves are softened by the textural qualities of the two pennisetum, both with brushstroke-like flower heads. While both are similar in terms of shape and purpose, they are in fact very different colours, each with exaggerated autumnal colourings. 'Rubrum', as its name suggests, boasts deep red foliage and striking soft rose flower spikes that complement the hydrangea, while 'Hameln' is much more earthy. Dark brown seeds of pennisetum 'Hameln' spread along the flower stalk, adding a neutral balance to the combo.

The hydrangea here is slightly different to the conventional type. The oak-leaved hydrangea does flower, but for me the foliage is where the excitement lies. The leaves are big, each up to 30cm (12in) long. The plant itself can grow up to 2m (6½ft) tall, so you want to leave ample space for it to grow and do its thing. Position this first, somewhere central where it can be allowed to develop into a sculptural piece.

The grasses can then be clustered in groups of five around the hydrangea. If you have one outrider from each grouping spaced slightly further away, it will help to break up the rigidity of any clumps.

TOP TIP Pennisetum 'Rubrum' can be tender, meaning that, in a very cold winter, it is unlikely to survive. If you have the luxury of any frost-free indoor space, such as a glasshouse, conservatory, or even a windowsill, into which you can bring these plants to protect them during the coldest of months, it is worth that extra effort. Lift them and bring them in before the first hard frosts, typically in early winter, and replant them back outside in late spring. Alternatively, you can treat them as annuals, replanting new plants each spring once the cold has passed.

54

PEAK INTEREST Autumn

TIME TO PLANT Autumn to spring

GROWING CONDITIONS Tolerant of most locations, these plants will grow where you plant them regardless of the conditions, making them ideal for those problematic corners that need greening up.

INGREDIENTS

Beautyberry 'Profusion' *Callicarpa bodinieri* var. *giraldii* 'Profusion' AGM, PFP

Garden privet *Ligustrum ovalifolium* PFP

Scruffy and unkept or wild and neglected are not usually qualities you want for plants in your garden. Yet, here is a combination that offers exactly that. Despite this, I would encourage you to consider finding a home for these plants somewhere in your outdoor space if you can.

There is plenty for us to enjoy here, from the autumnal foliage of the acer through to the vivid fluorescent purple berries of the callicarpa, the dancing movement of the panicum, and the dark, velvety fruits of the ligustrum. But these plants also provide our gardens with a home for beneficial insects and wildlife. So while this group of plants may be more unruly than others in this book, there is beauty in the wildness, both for us and for the food and shelter provided for our garden friends.

As this combination is designed to be rugged and wild, how you go about positioning the plants doesn't matter too much. Ultimately, the plants will knit together themselves, forming a tapestry of foliage and berries. Try to plant the taller individuals such as the acer and ligustrum towards the back and allow them space to mature.

The grasses can be woven throughout, emerging in late spring as the shrubs begin to leaf up, and the garden wakes for another year.

TOP TIP Leave well alone during the winter as this is when these plants provide food and shelter. Instead of tidying up those fallen leaves and sharpening up those borders, leave them be and celebrate the beauty in the decay that follows. The leaves will rot down of their own accord and enrich the soil, providing shelter before they do so. The berries on the shrubs will provide a vital food source, fallen twigs can be used for bird nests, and the grasses are ideal for insects to hide within.

Field maple *Acer campestre* PFP

Switch grass 'Prairie Sky' *Panicum virgatum* 'Prairie Sky'

55

PEAK INTEREST Spring and autumn

TIME TO PLANT Spring or autumn

GROWING CONDITIONS These plants are ideal for an open spot in your garden with good drainage and plenty of sun. They are happy to take centre stage as their resilient nature makes them ideal for those locations where other plants may struggle.

INGREDIENTS

Common medlar *Mespilus germanica* PFP

Switch grass 'Northwind' *Panicum virgatum* 'Northwind' AGM

Alpine strawberry *Fragaria vesca* PFP

Medlar is one of my favourite trees, but it's extremely underused. It's a fruit tree, producing autumn russet-coloured, round, hard fruits that resemble small apples. It also unfurls beautiful pure white blossom in spring, and offers incredible structure during the summer and winter. By far its best season is autumn, when it morphs into shades of butter yellow and cinnamon, resembling the colours of a perfectly cooked crumble crust.

The fragaria is a form of strawberry, but a wild version that would naturally be found in alpine mountainous conditions. While it does produce fruits, which are edible, they are small and insignificant; I grow this as an ornamental plant, as its daisylike flowers and crimson fruits add ground-cover jewels. Its foliage spreads and forms a mat over the ground, perfect for suppressing weeds and retaining moisture in the soil.

I have used panicum here to provide movement and mid-storey interest. It dances in the wind in the space between the fragaria and the medlar, offering seasonal interest, particularly in autumn.

The medlar is naturally the most dominant and structurally key plant here, so position it somewhere you can maximize its value, ideally where you can see it from a key window, or to frame a viewpoint. I have removed the lower branches to create a multistem effect. This makes the tree much more sculptural and interesting with very little effort. Plant the panicum and fragaria around the base. Both work best in drifts, so plant large groupings of them, ideally in odd numbers (three, five, or seven).

TOP TIP Medlar fruits are edible; in fact you can make jams and jellies from them. I leave mine for the birds and wildlife to feast upon. They get the fruits, while I enjoy the structure, shape, and blossom, which bring me just as much happiness as a jam or jelly.

56

PEAK INTEREST Autumn

TIME TO PLANT Spring or autumn

GROWING CONDITIONS These plants like good drainage and plenty of sun, so it's best to avoid any positions that may get wet in the winter. If you are concerned about winter wet, planting in a container will elevate their appearance and negate any concerns.

INGREDIENTS

Stag's horn sumach *Rhus typhina*

Orange New Zealand sedge *Carex testacea*

A simple, but hard-working duo, these two plants can offer an almost painterly appearance. The colourings and texture of the rhus and carex work effortlessly in tandem to create a display worthy of any gallery.

Rhus is a curious tree, producing large fronds of spear-shaped leaves that transition into magical reds and oranges as autumn arrives. The carex creates a carpet of billowing green tufts that also morph into illuminating oranges as the summer fades away. Together they light up the garden and provide one last pre-winter spectacle of fiery colours.

Personally, I think this is one of those combinations that is even better in a container than in the ground as this allows you to look up into the arching, woolly stems of the rhus. Whether you choose to plant in the ground or in a pot, use the rhus as the structural piece and plant the carex below en masse – the more the better.

Both require very little attention. Every few years you can carefully prune the rhus to keep it in shape, and comb through the carex, both tasks best done in early spring. Add some spring-flowering bulbs to extend the season of interest.

TOP TIP While it's beautiful, rhus can be a tad troublesome. It can be too eager to grow in some conditions and produces suckers, which are underground stems that run from the main tree and pop up where you don't really want them. To remove them, simply dig them out when young – they are harder to remove when they're older. Unfortunately, simply snipping them off at ground level won't work and they do require some digging. To avoid this entirely, grow in a pot or container to completely restrict their adventurous roots.

57

PEAK INTEREST Late summer and early autumn

TIME TO PLANT Spring or autumn

GROWING CONDITIONS Tolerant of most conditions, these plants favour drier areas with good drainage, avoiding the risk of any winter wet.

INGREDIENTS

Purple moor-grass 'Moorhexe' *Molinia caerulea* subsp. *caerulea* 'Moorhexe' AGM

Coneflower 'Goldsturm' *Rudbeckia fulgida* var. *sullivantii* 'Goldsturm' AGM, PFP

Maidenhair tree 'Globus' *Ginkgo biloba* 'Globus

Who says that bright colours need to be limited to the summer months? These plants provide the garden equivalent of the after party, keeping the energy going well into the shorter, colder days. They provide a much-needed burst of bright yellows at a time of year when we need them the most.

A ginkgo tree provides the structure here and, although I have used a dwarf ginkgo, it is still substantial enough to hold the planting together. An elegant tree, it comes alive most during the autumn, as its foliage transforms from a verdant green to illuminating yellow. As its leaves begin to fall it decorates the ground below with yellow confetti.

Rudbeckia is a plant I have used in multiple combinations throughout the book, as it's such a great doer and puts on a show all summer and autumn. With next to no intervention required, its bright yellow daisylike flowers are produced for months on end.

I have used the molinia here to provide texture and to act as a foil against the brighter colours of the other plants. Often the introduction of a grass such as molinia enables the other plants to shine even more, also adding an extra layer of interest particularly during the autumn as it turns a chestnut brown.

Start with the ginkgo as this will provide the structure. The rudbeckia produces an abundance of flowers, and works best planted in groups of three, five, or seven, depending on the size and space you have to fill. Drift the molinia between to act as a glue that will hold it all together.

In late winter cut the rudbeckia and molinia right back to the ground. Leave the ginkgo alone – this will only ever need light pruning every few years to keep its shape.

TOP TIP Ginkgo is an incredible tree, dating back to the Jurassic period and beyond. It has been around much longer than humans and will be around a long time after we have gone. Planting one in your garden is the equivalent of getting a dinosaur as a pet: it is truly special. I have chosen a smaller-growing variety here, as the normal species can grow particularly large. There are numerous types to choose from, but an important aspect to check is that you are buying a male tree. This may seem an odd thing to say, but female ginkgo produce the most rancid-smelling fruits that are best avoided; few trees create such impressively repulsive fruit.

58

PEAK INTEREST Summer and autumn

TIME TO PLANT Late spring

GROWING CONDITIONS These plants prefer a sheltered spot in the garden, somewhere tucked away to protect them from any extreme wind and deep frost pockets.

INGREDIENTS

Japanese aralia *Fatsia japonica* AGM, PFP

Necklace vine *Muehlenbeckia complexa*

Canna 'Cleopatra' *Canna* 'Cleopatra' AGM

Canna 'Durban' *Canna* 'Durban'

This simple but dominating collection of foliage plants is all about the leaves. Without a flower in sight, you can create drama and intensity with just a mixture of large, jungly leaves of varying shapes and sizes. The canna plants have large foliage similar to banana leaves, in greens and reds, and add a real touch of the exotic to the combination. While they do flower, I am much more interested in their foliage here.

The fatsia is the largest plant, so start with that. They can grow rather large – up to 3m (10ft) tall if left alone – although they are easy enough to keep in check by pruning every couple of years. You won't need many to make an impressive display.

The canna need planting next. They are a little more work than the other plants as they are not frost hardy. They will tolerate small frosts, but anything too heavy risks killing the plant. I get away with planting them in a sheltered position in London, but in a more exposed spot, it is worth digging them up each autumn. Cut back the foliage, dig up the plant, and bash off all the soil. Find a dry, frost-free, sheltered spot somewhere under cover or indoors, that doesn't get too warm, to rehouse them during the winter. It's a little extra work, but well worth it for the beauty they provide.

The muehlenbeckia can be positioned in the gaps among the other plants, where it will naturally sprawl and tumble, finding its own way through the planting. It is evergreen, and can be left alone. The only time to trim it is if it is starting to grow too large for its space.

TOP TIP If planting in a container, as I have here, get creative. Often the cheapest, most random vessels make for the best planters. Here I have upcycled an old, galvanized steel water tank I found online. In its former life, it was used to store water on a farm, but it's now home to an extravagant, foliage-heavy display of garden tropics. I think the industrial chic style of it works brilliantly against the large leaves.

59

PEAK INTEREST Autumn

TIME TO PLANT Spring or autumn

GROWING CONDITIONS The acer needs a sheltered position, as it can be vulnerable to windy or exposed spots, which can cause its foliage to scorch and go crispy. This group is best in a corner or against a wall that will provide protection. They need soil with good drainage so they don't get too wet over the winter period.

INGREDIENTS

Japanese maple 'Dissectum'
Acer palmatum **'Dissectum'**

Japanese forest grass *Hakonechloa macra* AGM

I couldn't write a book about plant combinations and not include the iconic acer, Japanese maple. This is a stalwart of the garden, and it's not hard to see why as its foliage transforms in autumn into a duvet of crimson red, a billowing blur of autumnal magic.

The hakonechloa is used to underplant, creating a skirt of frothing green goodness that spills out from beneath the majesty of the acer. Together they create a Japanese-inspired palette that I have deliberately kept restrained. The addition of more plants here would only detract from the natural beauty they offer.

Position the acer first, somewhere sheltered but equally somewhere you can really appreciate the structure and beauty it will add to your outdoor space – perhaps framed by a window or visible from a location where you can perch and enjoy it. The hakonechloa can be planted in large clumps or swathes. It looks best en masse, so don't be afraid to plant more than you think you will need.

The hakonechloa can be left during the winter as its golden, crispy foliage is still beautiful, particularly as it sparkles in a strong frost. It also provides an essential habitat in which beneficial insects can shelter during the harshest months. In late winter cut it right back to the ground.

The acer requires next to no pruning or maintenance other than the removal of any obviously dead or damaged branches.

TOP TIP While this duo certainly can be planted in the garden, I feel that it is enhanced and elevated by planting it in a container. This will raise the hakonechloa more into view and, with a little clever pruning, you could lift the branches of the acer to enable you to see in and through its framework of branches.

60

PEAK INTEREST Late summer and autumn

TIME TO PLANT Spring

GROWING CONDITIONS This duo are lovers of full sun and good drainage, so try to ensure that they have room to grow and shine without much shade or overhanging coverage. They can tolerate decent levels of moisture, but don't want to sit wet over the winter.

INGREDIENTS

Chinese fountain grass 'Hameln' *Pennisetum alopecuroides* 'Hameln' AGM

White wood aster *Eurybia divaricata*

It is always surprising the impact and power just two plants can have when they work well together. Less is more so often in planting, and this simplicity can be used to create real magic.

Pennisetum is one of my favourite grasses, adding drama and impact – something not many other grasses achieve. Architectural in its own right, it produces striking flower spikes, not flowers as you would typically expect to see them, but more brushlike and characterful. As the seasons progress and the cold arrives, the early morning frost catches these beautifully.

The eurybia produces thousands of delicate, white, starlike daisies, creating a flowering swarm. When in full bloom the impressive quantity practically smothers the plant. Despite its floriferous nature, it is remarkably gentle and romantic, floating in the slightest of breezes among the pennisetum.

This forgiving pair of plants will reward you in abundance no matter how you position them. Whether it's a couple of each plant in a stylish container, or large drifts in a bigger space, they are dynamic and hardworking. I would try to intermingle them as best you can, as the way the eurybia flowers dance through the flower heads of the pennisetum is magical.

TOP TIP These two plants are late starters and, other than an abundance of foliage, there is not too much to see until late summer. To stretch out the season of interest, you can either use these plants under a larger tree or structural plant – perhaps phillyrea (narrow-leaved privet) or olive – or combine them with an earlier-flowering combination from the spring or summer chapters, such as combination 17.

61

PEAK INTEREST Year round

TIME TO PLANT Spring or autumn

GROWING CONDITIONS All three of these plants will grow just about anywhere, but will most enjoy a slightly damp, sheltered spot that avoids excessive summer heat or drought.

INGREDIENTS

West Himalayan birch *Betula utilis* subsp. *jacquemontii*

Scaly male fern *Dryopteris affinis* AGM

Tree ivy *Hedera helix* 'Arborescens' PFP

An iconic tree, the simple birch is a staple of many gardens and landscapes. This is due in no small part to its extreme versatility, eagerness to grow, and the impressive stature it provides. This variety is particularly elegant, with pure white flaking bark that provides year-round interest. In autumn, its foliage takes on a rich golden shade of yellow.

Ivy can be a problem-child of the garden, with some species becoming rampant and taking over, earning it a bad reputation. This is a much more well-behaved, non-climbing version that produces squat evergreen shrubs that bear clusters of dark velvet berries in the winter.

The dryopteris is a semi-evergreen fern, so continues to provide interest well into the winter, and offers low coverage along the ground.

Individually, these are all great plants that easily deserve a spot in any garden, and collectively the balance between the vivid white and verdant greens provides a striking yet calming combination.

The birch comes first. Position this somewhere it will have the most impact, and, as it grows and matures, somewhere it can provide dappled shade and shelter in the summer. The ivy is the next largest, structural in its own right, and providing dumpling-like mounds of evergreen structure. You won't need many of these to add a lot of impact – I have only used three here, and that's plenty.

The dryopteris is then used as a filler, to add low ground-cover interest. Plant this in clusters or to fill gaps between the birch and ivy; personally I prefer to keep the planting restrained, so less is more with these.

TOP TIP This may sound extremely odd, but stay with me here. Arguably the biggest feature of this combination is the pure white bark of the birch. One of the wonderful aspects of any birch tree is that it naturally sheds its older bark to reveal fresh bark underneath. Each winter, I like to clean my birch trunks. Yes, really. Using some lukewarm water and a sponge, you can remove any algae or dirt that may have accumulated over the course of the year, ensuring that during the winter when the bark is most visible, it looks its absolute best. You would do the same with furniture inside your house, so why not enhance something so beautiful in the garden?

PEAK INTEREST Spring and autumn

TIME TO PLANT Spring or autumn

GROWING CONDITIONS A woodland combination that prefers a shadier position, this is perfect for those sheltered spots in the garden where other plants may struggle.

INGREDIENTS

Paperbark maple *Acer griseum* AGM

You may recognize this tree from the Spring chapter, where I used it to showcase the fresh young green foliage as it first appears, contrasting against the bronze peeling bark (see combination 2). Here, two seasons later, this acer is still showing off, this time with dazzling autumnal foliage. This brilliant tree provides year-round interest effortlessly.

Here I have used a restrained palette of evergreens that will provide interest throughout the winter. The fern and nandina are both strong performers, unsung heroes of the garden, and yet, in the autumn, they add a little extra pizzazz as they produce burgundy-coloured new growth that complements the autumnal performance of the acer.

Common rasp-fern *Doodia media*

The acer takes centre stage here, providing form and structure. Its sculptural qualities are only enhanced as the foliage falls, leaving exposed trunks of peeling bark. Plant this where its structure can be best appreciated, be that in a container or at a focal point in your garden.

The nandina and doodia create a verdant layer below. Left unchecked, the nandina will grow into a largish shrub, so only a few are required; in fact here I have only used one, which is ample. The doodia can be used a little more generously, but you don't need to use too many to create the desired effect.

All three plants can be left alone during winter, and only infrequent pruning in spring is required to keep them in shape over the years. In addition, remove any dead leaves, stems, and branches to keep the plants healthy.

TOP TIP Since I've used this tree in both spring (see combination 2) and autumn, you can see how the variation of underplanting can transform the way it works within a space. If you can't decide which one you prefer, why not mix them up a little and create a fusion of both combinations?

Heavenly bamboo *Nandina domestica* OBSESSED

63

PEAK INTEREST Autumn and winter

TIME TO PLANT Spring or autumn

GROWING CONDITIONS These plants are happy to grow in most conditions, sunny or shady, but try to ensure good drainage.

INGREDIENTS

Winter-flowering cherry 'Autumnalis'
Prunus × *subhirtella* 'Autumnalis'

Heucherella 'Sweet Tea' × *Heucherella* 'Sweet Tea'

Orange New Zealand sedge *Carex testacea*

The autumnal foliage of the prunus lights up the garden with a blaze of fiery burnt oranges, rusty reds, and golden amber. By underplanting it with carex and heucherella, I have leaned into this autumnal extravaganza, embracing the bold colours that this magical season does so well.

Blossom is synonymous with spring, so it seems inconceivable to imagine a flowering cherry during autumn and winter. This rogue prunus didn't read the rules, though, and produces white flowers between mid-autumn and early spring. Is it extremely late, or very early? Either way, its joyful blossoms are a welcome addition to the colder months when most other plants are beginning to die down, keeping the garden alive and vibrant.

Position the prunus somewhere it can have the space to establish. Consider it a sculptural piece, and give it the opportunity to maximize its shape and structure and ultimately, the dappled shade it will provide. Plant the carex and heucherella underneath. I prefer to group them together into threes or fives of each plant as I think these larger drifts carry more impact.

Both the carex and heucherella are evergreen, and can be left alone during the winter. In spring, give them a tidy up to remove any dead foliage.

TOP TIP You may wish to introduce other plants for more spring and summer interest. For me, some fiery spring bulbs such as the tulip 'Queen of the Night' or the wild *Tulipa sylvestris* would make great additions, followed by dashes of cosmos to brighten the summer.

64

PEAK INTEREST Spring to autumn

TIME TO PLANT Any season

GROWING CONDITIONS These plants are extremely versatile and tolerant of most places and conditions, as long as the ground is relatively free draining. Yew, in particular, don't like sitting in wet soil, especially over the winter.

INGREDIENTS

Common yew *Taxus baccata* AGM

Japanese forest grass *Hakonechloa macra* AGM

Mexican fleabane *Erigeron karvinskianus* AGM, PFP

Arguably this is one of the simplest combinations in this book, yet its timeless beauty and versatile nature makes it a natural winner for gardens of all sizes and styles. The balance between structure through the tightly clipped yew and the frothy goodness of the hakonechloa and erigeron creates a perfect, cohesive display. You will see many garden designers using this trio and, as it is such a restrained palette, you can incorporate it quickly, and easily, in your own garden. Erigeron flowers right through from mid-spring to mid-autumn, making it one of those truly special plants that just doesn't know when to stop.

The form is provided here by the smooth curves of the yew. If left untouched it grows into a majestic tree but, with some gentle pruning, it can be shaped into balls, as we have here, a hedge, or just about anything you could possibly imagine. I prefer the simplicity of the balls, but feel free to experiment.

Start with the yew, which is the glue that holds this all together. It's important to get the positioning right. A trio works well, but you can adjust numbers to match the size of the space. Plant both the hakonechloa and erigeron in the gaps around the yew, where they will naturally thrill and spill, creating a fluffed skirt around the edges.

The yew balls look their very best when tightly clipped. The more you clip them, the tighter the foliage will become. In time, as they get denser and denser, you can wobble them like mounds of set jelly. I clip my topiary twice a year and find this to be more than adequate. However, there is nothing stopping you doing it more frequently if desired. Cut back the erigeron and hakonechloa in late winter, and they will soon shoot back.

TOP TIP Use a variety of sizes of yew to create a mounded effect. Here I have used three different sizes, the largest 80cm (32in) wide, then 60cm (24in), then 40cm (16in). Varying the sizes creates a much more sculpted appearance.

PLANT COMBINATION GUIDE

For those of you who want all the planting information – soil types, light levels, ultimate heights, etc. – it's here. We have collated all that technical data into this plant combination guide for you to cross-reference against any combinations – or individual plants – you like the look of. Using these details will help to give you peace of mind that these plants will grow and thrive in your own garden. They are listed by combination number, 1-64, across spring, summer, and autumn.

Combination	Ingredients (Common Name)	Ingredients (Latin Name)	Awards	Plant Type
1	Sage Love and Wishes	Salvia Love and Wishes ('Serendip6')	PFP	Perennial
	Dark purple Siberian melic	Melica altissima 'Atropurpurea'		Grass
	Peony 'Sarah Bernhardt'	Paeonia lactiflora 'Sarah Bernhardt'	AGM	Perennial
2	Paperbark maple	Acer griseum	AGM	Tree
	Mrs Robb's bonnet	Euphorbia amygdaloides var. robbiae	AGM, PFP	Perennial
	Summer snowflake 'Gravetye Giant'	Leucojum aestivum 'Gravetye Giant'	AGM	Perennial
	Large-flowered barrenwort	Epimedium grandiflorum		Perennial
	Male fern	Dryopteris filix-mas	AGM	Fern
	Copper shield fern	Dryopteris erythrosora	AGM	Fern
3	Meadow rue 'Black Stockings'	Thalictrum 'Black Stockings'	AGM	Perennial
	Avens 'Prinses Juliana'	Geum 'Prinses Juliana'	AGM	Perennial
	Snow rush	Luzula nivea		Grass
	Spurge 'Black Pearl'	Euphorbia characias 'Black Pearl'	PFP	Perennial
4	Pineapple guava	Feijoa sellowiana		Shrub
	Mexican feather grass	Stipa tenuissima	AGM	Grass
	Mexican fleabane	Erigeron karvinskianus	AGM, PFP	Perennial
	Iris 'Kent Pride'	Iris 'Kent Pride'		Perennial
	Mediterranean spurge	Euphorbia characias subsp. wulfenii	PFP	Perennial
	Thyme 'Albiflorus'	Thymus praecox 'Albiflorus'	PFP	Perennial

PLANT HARDINESS KEY Hardiness rating systems help us to determine what levels of cold weather plants can tolerate. Every plant can withstand different levels of cold, with some being much more resilient than others. We have used the RHS's hardiness system to indicate the hardiness of each plant in this index. While most of the plants in this book are very hardy, this system allows you to check the cold tolerance of each plant in a simple and easy to navigate way. The USDA zone numbers (below) are used in the United States to indicate hardiness. The temperatures indicated here are minimum temperatures.

Hardiness Rating	Temperature Range	USDA Zone
H3	-5 to 1°C (23 to 34°F)	9b/10a
H4	-10 to -5°C (14 to 23°F)	8b/9a
H5	-15 to -10°C (5 to 14°F)	7b/8a
H6	-20 to -15°C (-4 to 5°F)	6b/7a
H7	Colder than -20°C (-4°F)	6a-1

Height	Spread	Soil	Soil pH	Position	Exposure	Hardiness
0.5–1m (20–39in)	0.1–0.5m (4–20in)	Chalk, loam, sand	Any	Full sun	Sheltered	H3
1–1.5m (3–5ft)	0.1–0.5m (4–20in)	Any	Any	Full sun or partial shade	Exposed or sheltered	H6
0.5–1m (20–39in)	0.5–1m (20–39in)	Any	Any	Full sun or partial shade	Sheltered	H6
8–12m (26–39ft)	4–8m (13–26ft)	Any	Any	Full sun or partial shade	Sheltered	H5
0.1–0.5m (4–20in)	1–1.5m (3–5ft)	Chalk, loam, sand	Any	Any	Exposed or sheltered	H6
0.5–1m (20–39in)	0.1–0.5m (4–20in)	Any	Any	Full sun	Exposed or sheltered	H7
0.1–0.5m (4–20in)	0.1–0.5m (4–20in)	Chalk, loam, sand	Acid or neutral	Partial shade	Sheltered	H5
1–1.5m (3–5ft)	0.5–1m (20–39in)	Any	Any	Full shade or partial shade	Exposed or sheltered	H7
0.5–1m (20–39in)	0.5–1m (20–39in)	Any	Any	Any	Sheltered	H4
1.5–2.5m (5–8ft)	0.1–0.5m (4–20in)	Chalk, clay, loam	Any	Full sun or partial shade	Sheltered	H7
0.1–0.5m (4–20in)	0.1–0.5m (4–20in)	Chalk, loam, sand	Any	Full sun	Exposed or sheltered	H7
0.5–1m (20–39in)	0.1–0.5m (4–20in)	Chalk, loam, sand	Any	Full shade or partial shade	Exposed or sheltered	H5
0.5–1m (20–39in)	0.5–1m (20–39in)	Chalk, loam, sand	Any	Full sun	Sheltered	H4
1.5–2.5m (5–8ft)	1.5–2.5m (5–8ft)	Chalk, loam, sand	Any	Full sun	Sheltered	H3
0.5–1m (20–39in)	0.1–0.5m (4–20in)	Any	Any	Full sun	Exposed or sheltered	H4
0.1–0.5m (4–20in)	0.5–1m (20–39in)	Any	Any	Full sun	Exposed	H5
0.5–1m (20–39in)	0.1–0.5m (4–20in)	Loam, sand	Acid or neutral	Full sun	Exposed or sheltered	H7
1–1.5m (3–5ft)	1–1.5m (3–5ft)	Chalk, loam, sand	Any	Full sun	Sheltered	H4
Up to 10cm (4in)	0.1–0.5m (4–20in)	Chalk, loam, sand	Alkaline or neutral	Full sun	Exposed or sheltered	H4

Combination	Ingredients (Common Name)	Ingredients (Latin Name)	Awards	Plant Type
5	White pasqueflower Red pasqueflower Mexican feather grass Bearded iris	*Pulsatilla vulgaris* 'Alba' *Pulsatilla rubra* *Stipa tenuissima* *Iris* 'Sable Night'	 AGM 	Perennial Perennial Grass Perennial
6	Hard fern Plume thistle 'Atropurpureum' Redvein enkianthus Dusky cranesbill Male fern	*Blechnum spicant* *Cirsium rivulare* 'Atropurpureum' *Enkianthus campanulatus* *Geranium phaeum* *Dryopteris filix-mas*	AGM AGM, PFP AGM PFP AGM	Fern Perennial Shrub Perennial Fern
7	Balkan clary 'Caradonna' Bronze fennel Garden catmint 'Purrsian Blue'	*Salvia nemorosa* 'Caradonna' *Foeniculum vulgare* 'Purpureum' *Nepeta* × *faassenii* 'Purrsian Blue'	AGM, PFP PFP AGM, PFP	Perennial Perennial Perennial
8	Delavay osmanthus Allium 'Mount Everest' Pheasant's tail grass	*Osmanthus delavayi* *Allium stipitatum* 'Mount Everest' *Anemanthele lessoniana*	AGM AGM, PFP AGM	Shrub Bulb Grass
9	Hazel Dusky cranesbill 'Lily Lovell' Copper shield fern Common columbine Alpine wood fern	*Corylus avellana* *Geranium phaeum* 'Lily Lovell' *Dryopteris erythrosora* *Aquilegia vulgaris* *Dryopteris wallichiana*	 PFP AGM PFP AGM	Shrub / Tree Perennial Fern Perennial Fern
10	Plantain lily 'Devon Green' Giant blue hosta Plantain lily 'Krossa Regal' Bloody cranesbill 'Album'	*Hosta* 'Devon Green' *Hosta sieboldiana* var. *elegans* *Hosta* 'Krossa Regal' *Geranium sanguineum* 'Album'	AGM AGM AGM AGM, PFP	Perennial Perennial Perennial Perennial
11	Male fern Vial's primrose Goat's beard 'Horatio' Bee's primrose Japanese primrose 'Alba'	*Dryopteris filix-mas* *Primula vialii* *Aruncus* 'Horatio' *Primula beesiana* *Primula japonica* 'Alba'	AGM AGM AGM 	Fern Perennial Perennial Perennial Perennial
12	Narrow-leaved mock privet Purple moor-grass	*Phillyrea angustifolia* *Molinia caerulea* subsp. *caerulea* 'Poul Petersen'	 AGM	Shrub Grass
13	Aralia Green Fingers Cappadocian navelwort 'Cherry Ingram' Lily of the valley Tellima 'Forest Frost' Hard fern	*Fatsia polycarpa* Green Fingers *Omphalodes cappadocica* 'Cherry Ingram' *Convallaria majalis* *Tellima grandiflora* 'Forest Frost' *Blechnum spicant*	 AGM AGM PFP AGM	Shrub Perennial Perennial Perennial Fern
14	Foxglove 'Sutton's Apricot' Marsh spurge Baltic parsley Bear's breech	*Digitalis purpurea* 'Sutton's Apricot' *Euphorbia palustris* *Cenolophium denudatum* *Acanthus mollis*	PFP AGM, PFP AGM 	Perennial Perennial Perennial Perennial

Height	Spread	Soil	Soil pH	Position	Exposure	Hardiness
0.1–0.5m (4–20in)	0.1–0.5m (4–20in)	Chalk, loam, sand	Acid or neutral	Full sun	Exposed	H5
0.1–0.5m (4–20in)	0.1–0.5m (4–20in)	Chalk, loam, sand	Any	Full sun	Exposed or sheltered	H5
0.5–1m (20–39in)	0.1–0.5m (4–20in)	Any	Any	Full sun	Exposed or sheltered	H4
0.5–1m (20–39in)	0.1–0.5m (4–20in)	Loam, sand	Acid or neutral	Full sun	Exposed	H7
0.1–0.5m (4–20in)	0.1–0.5m (4–20in)	Clay, loam	Acid or neutral	Full shade or partial shade	Exposed or sheltered	H6
1–1.5m (3–5ft)	0.1–0.5m (4–20in)	Chalk, loam, sand	Any	Full sun	Exposed or sheltered	H7
2.5–4m (8–13ft)	2.5–4m (8–13ft)	Clay, loam, sand	Acid or neutral	Full sun or partial shade	Sheltered	H5
0.5–1m (20–39in)	0.1–0.5m (4–20in)	Any	Any	Any	Sheltered	H7
1–1.5m (3–5ft)	0.5–1m (20–39in)	Any	Any	Full shade or partial shade	Exposed or sheltered	H7
0.1–0.5m (4–20in)	0.1–0.5m (4–20in)	Chalk, loam, sand	Any	Full sun or partial shade	Exposed or sheltered	H7
1.5–2.5m (5–8ft)	0.5–1m (20–39in)	Any	Any	Full sun	Sheltered	H5
0.1–0.5m (4–20in)	0.5–1m (20–39in)	Chalk, loam, sand	Any	Full sun	Exposed or sheltered	H7
2.5–4m (8–13ft)	2.5–4m (8–13ft)	Any	Any	Full sun or partial shade	Exposed or sheltered	H5
1–1.5m (3–5ft)	0.1–0.5m (4–20in)	Any	Any	Full sun	Sheltered	H5
0.5–1m (20–39in)	1–1.5m (3–5ft)	Any	Any	Full sun or partial shade	Exposed or sheltered	H4
4–8m (13–26ft)	4–8m (13–26ft)	Chalk, loam, sand	Alkaline or neutral	Full sun or partial shade	Exposed or sheltered	H6
0.5–1m (20–39in)	0.1–0.5m (4–20in)	Any	Any	Any	Exposed or sheltered	H7
0.5–1m (20–39in)	0.5–1m (20–39in)	Any	Any	Any	Sheltered	H4
0.5–1m (20–39in)	0.1–0.5m (4–20in)	Loam, sand	Any	Full sun or partial shade	Exposed or sheltered	H7
0.5–1m (20–39in)	0.5–1m (20–39in)	Any	Any	Full shade or partial shade	Sheltered	H5
0.1–0.5m (4–20in)	0.5–1m (20–39in)	Clay, loam	Any	Partial shade	Sheltered	H7
0.5–1m (20–39in)	0.5–1m (20–39in)	Clay, loam	Acid or neutral	Partial shade	Sheltered	H7
1–1.5m (3–5ft)	1–1.5m (3–5ft)	Clay, loam	Acid or neutral	Partial shade	Sheltered	H7
0.1–0.5m (4–20in)	0.5–1m (20–39in)	Any	Any	Full sun or partial shade	Exposed or sheltered	H7
1–1.5m (3–5ft)	0.5–1m (20–39in)	Any	Any	Full shade or partial shade	Exposed or sheltered	H7
0.1–0.5m (4–20in)	0.1–0.5m (4–20in)	Loam	Acid or neutral	Partial shade	Sheltered	H5
1–1.5m (3–5ft)	0.5–1m (20–39in)	Clay, loam	Any	Full sun or partial shade	Exposed or sheltered	H6
0.1–0.5m (4–20in)	0.1–0.5m (4–20in)	Clay, loam	Acid or neutral	Full sun or partial shade	Sheltered	H6
0.5–1m (20–39in)	0.1–0.5m (4–20in)	Clay, loam	Acid or neutral	Partial shade	Sheltered	H6
2.5–4m (8–13ft)	1.5–2.5m (5–8ft)	Sand	Any	Full sun or partial shade	Exposed or sheltered	H5
0.5–1m (20–39in)	0.1–0.5m (4–20in)	Clay, loam, sand	Acid or neutral	Full sun or partial shade	Exposed or sheltered	H7
2.5–4m (8–13ft)	1.5–2.5m (5–8ft)	Any	Any	Full sun	Sheltered	H3
0.1–0.5m (4–20in)	0.1–0.5m (4–20in)	Any	Any	Partial shade	Sheltered	H5
0.1–0.5m (4–20in)	0.1–0.5m (4–20in)	Clay, loam	Any	Full shade or partial shade	Sheltered	H7
0.1–0.5m (4–20in)	0.1–0.5m (4–20in)	Any	Any	Any	Exposed or sheltered	H6
0.1–0.5m (4–20in)	0.1–0.5m (4–20in)	Clay, loam	Acid or neutral	Full sun or partial shade	Exposed or sheltered	H6
1–1.5m (3–5ft)	0.1–0.5m (4–20in)	Any	Any	Any	Sheltered	H7
0.5–1m (20–39in)	0.5–1m (20–39in)	Clay, loam	Any	Full sun	Exposed or sheltered	H7
1–1.5m (3–5ft)	0.1–0.5m (4–20in)	Any	Any	Full sun or partial shade	Exposed or sheltered	H6
1–1.5m (3–5ft)	1–1.5m (3–5ft)	Chalk, loam, sand	Any	Any	Exposed or sheltered	H6

Combination	Ingredients (Common Name)	Ingredients (Latin Name)	Awards	Plant Type
15	Peony 'Sarah Bernhardt' Peony 'Coral Charm'	*Paeonia lactiflora* 'Sarah Bernhardt' *Paeonia* 'Coral Charm'	AGM AGM	Perennial Perennial
16	Chinese dogwood Copper shield fern 'Brilliance' Shaggy wood fern Soft shield fern	*Cornus kousa* var. *chinensis* *Dryopteris erythrosora* 'Brilliance' *Dryopteris cycadina* *Polystichum setiferum*	AGM AGM AGM	Tree Fern Fern Fern
17	Yarrow 'Moonshine' Wood sage 'Viola Klose' Catmint 'Summer Magic'	*Achillea* 'Moonshine' *Salvia* × *sylvestris* 'Viola Klose' *Nepeta grandiflora* 'Summer Magic'	AGM, PFP AGM, PFP AGM, PFP	Perennial Perennial Perennial
18	Copper shield fern Siberian iris 'Caesar's Brother' Soft shield fern 'Herrenhausen'	*Dryopteris erythrosora* *Iris* 'Caesar's Brother' *Polystichum setiferum* 'Herrenhausen'	AGM	Fern Perennial Fern
19	Allium 'Mont Blanc' Macedonian scabious Eulalia 'Gracillimus'	*Allium* 'Mont Blanc' *Knautia macedonica* *Miscanthus sinensis* 'Gracillimus'	PFP PFP	Bulb Perennial Grass
20	Japanese primrose 'Alba' Rhubarb 'Atrosanguineum' Hard fern Plantain lily 'Devon Green' Plantain lily 'Krossa Regal'	*Primula japonica* 'Alba' *Rheum palmatum* 'Atrosanguineum' *Blechnum spicant* *Hosta* 'Devon Green' *Hosta* 'Krossa Regal'	 AGM AGM AGM	Perennial Perennial Fern Perennial Perennial
21	Yarrow 'Lilac Beauty' Purple loosestrife 'Feuerkerze' Lobelia 'Hadspen Purple' Sage Pink Amistad	*Achillea millefolium* 'Lilac Beauty' *Lythrum salicaria* 'Feuerkerze' *Lobelia* × *speciosa* 'Hadspen Purple' *Salvia* Pink Amistad ('Arggr17011')	PFP AGM, PFP PFP	Perennial Perennial Perennial Perennial
22	Hydrangea Strong Annabelle Lady's mantle Catmint 'Six Hills Giant'	*Hydrangea arborescens* Strong Annabelle *Alchemilla mollis* *Nepeta* 'Six Hills Giant'	AGM AGM AGM, PFP	Shrub Perennial Perennial
23	Anemone Regal Swan Purple moor-grass 'Heidebraut' Red bistort 'Superba'	*Anemone* Regal Swan ('Macane044') *Molinia caerulea* subsp. *caerulea* 'Heidebraut' *Bistorta officinalis* 'Superba'	 AGM	Perennial Grass Perennial
24	Bronze fennel Montbretia 'Lucifer' Purple moor-grass 'Heidebraut'	*Foeniculum vulgare* 'Purpureum' *Crocosmia* 'Lucifer' *Molinia caerulea* subsp. *caerulea* 'Heidebraut'	PFP AGM	Perennial Perennial Grass
25	Chinese fountain grass 'Hameln' Japanese anemone 'Whirlwind'	*Pennisetum alopecuroides* 'Hameln' *Anemone* × *hybrida* 'Whirlwind'	AGM	Grass Perennial
26	Switch grass 'Prairie Sky' Blue eryngo Perovskia 'Blue Spire'	*Panicum virgatum* 'Prairie Sky' *Eryngium planum* *Salvia* 'Blue Spire'	 PFP AGM, PFP	Grass Perennial Perennial

Height	Spread	Soil	Soil pH	Position	Exposure	Hardiness
0.5–1m (20–39in)	0.5–1m (20–39in)	Any	Any	Full sun or partial shade	Sheltered	H6
0.5–1m (20–39in)	0.5–1m (20–39in)	Clay, loam, sand	Any	Full sun or partial shade	Sheltered	H6
4–8m (13–26ft)	4–8m (13–26ft)	Clay, loam, sand	Any	Full sun or partial shade	Exposed or sheltered	H6
0.5–1m (20–39in)	0.5–1m (20–39in)	Any	Any	Full shade or partial shade	Sheltered	H5
0.5–1m (20–39in)	0.1–0.5m (4–20in)	Any	Any	Full shade or partial shade	Sheltered	H4
1–1.5m (3–5ft)	0.5–1m (20–39in)	Any	Any	Full shade or partial shade	Exposed or sheltered	H7
0.5–1m (20–39in)	0.1–0.5m (4–20in)	Chalk, loam, sand	Any	Full sun	Exposed	H7
0.1–0.5m (4–20in)	0.1–0.5m (4–20in)	Chalk, loam, sand	Any	Full sun	Exposed or sheltered	H7
0.5–1m (20–39in)	0.5–1m (20–39in)	Chalk, loam, sand	Any	Full sun	Exposed	H7
0.5–1m (20–39in)	0.5–1m (20–39in)	Any	Any	Any	Sheltered	H4
0.5–1m (20–39in)	0.1–0.5m (4–20in)	Any	Any	Full sun or partial shade	Exposed or sheltered	H7
0.5–1m (20–39in)	0.5–1m (20–39in)	Clay, loam, sand	Any	Full shade or partial shade	Exposed or sheltered	H7
0.5–1m (20–39in)	0.1–0.5m (4–20in)	Any	Any	Full sun	Sheltered	H5
0.5–1m (20–39in)	0.1–0.5m (4–20in)	Chalk, loam, sand	Alkaline or neutral	Full sun	Exposed or sheltered	H7
1–1.8m (3–6ft)	0.5–1m (20–39in)	Any	Any	Full sun	Exposed or sheltered	H6
0.5–1m (20–39in)	0.1–0.5m (4–20in)	Clay, loam	Acid or neutral	Partial shade	Sheltered	H6
1.5–2.5m (5–8ft)	1–1.5m (3–5ft)	Clay, loam	Acid or neutral	Full sun or partial shade	Exposed or sheltered	H6
0.1–0.5m (4–20in)	0.1–0.5m (4–20in)	Clay, loam	Acid or neutral	Full sun or partial shade	Exposed or sheltered	H6
0.1–0.5m (4–20in)	0.5–1m (20–39in)	Clay, loam	Any	Partial shade	Sheltered	H7
1–1.5m (3–5ft)	1–1.5m (3–5ft)	Clay, loam	Acid or neutral	Partial shade	Sheltered	H7
0.5–1m (20–39in)	0.5–1m (20–39in)	Chalk, loam, sand	Any	Full sun	Exposed or sheltered	H7
1–1.5m (3–5ft)	0.1–0.5m (4–20in)	Clay, loam	Any	Full sun	Exposed or sheltered	H7
0.5–1m (20–39in)	0.1–0.5m (4–20in)	Any	Any	Full sun or partial shade	Exposed or sheltered	H5
1.5m (5ft)	0.6m (24in)	Chalk, loam, sand	Any	Full sun or partial shade	Sheltered	H3
1.5–2.5m (5–8ft)	1–1.5m (3–5ft)	Chalk, loam, sand	Acid or neutral	Full sun or partial shade	Exposed or sheltered	H6
0.1–0.5m (4–20in)	0.1–0.5m (4–20in)	Any	Any	Any	Exposed or sheltered	H7
0.5–1m (20–39in)	0.5–1m (20–39in)	Any	Any	Full sun or partial shade	Exposed or sheltered	H7
0.1–0.5m (4–20in)	0.1–0.5m (4–20in)	Chalk, clay, loam	Any	Partial shade	Exposed or sheltered	H4
1–1.5m (3–5ft)	0.1–0.5m (4–20in)	Any	Acid or neutral	Full sun or partial shade	Exposed or sheltered	H7
0.5–1m (20–39in)	0.5–1m (20–39in)	Any	Any	Full sun or partial shade	Exposed or sheltered	H7
1.5–1.8m (5–6ft)	0.5–1m (20–39in)	Any	Any	Full sun	Sheltered	H5
1.5–2.5m (5–8ft)	0.1–0.5m (4–20in)	Any	Any	Full sun or partial shade	Exposed or sheltered	H5
1–1.5m (3–5ft)	0.1–0.5m (4–20in)	Any	Acid or neutral	Full sun or partial shade	Exposed or sheltered	H7
0.5–1m (20–39in)	0.5–1m (20–39in)	Chalk, loam, sand	Any	Full sun	Sheltered	H3
0.5–1m (20–39in)	0.1–0.5m (4–20in)	Any	Any	Full sun or partial shade	Exposed or sheltered	H7
1–1.5m (3–5ft)	0.5–1m (20–39in)	Any	Any	Full sun	Exposed or sheltered	H5
0.5–1m (20–39in)	0.1–0.5m (4–20in)	Chalk, loam, sand	Any	Full sun	Sheltered	H5
1–1.5m (3–5ft)	0.5–1m (20–39in)	Chalk, loam, sand	Any	Full sun	Exposed or sheltered	H5

Combination	Ingredients (Common Name)	Ingredients (Latin Name)	Awards	Plant Type
27	Purple top	*Verbena bonariensis*	AGM, PFP	Perennial
	Purple moor-grass	*Molinia caerulea*		Grass
	Sweet pea 'Mrs Collier'	*Lathyrus odoratus* 'Mrs Collier'	AGM	Annual
	Sweet pea 'Black Knight'	*Lathyrus odoratus* 'Black Knight'		Annual
	Cosmea 'Purity'	*Cosmos bipinnatus* 'Purity'	PFP	Annual
	Cosmea 'Apricotta'	*Cosmos bipinnatus* 'Apricotta'		Annual
	Cosmea 'Rubenza'	*Cosmos bipinnatus* 'Rubenza'	AGM, PFP	Annual
28	Bowman's root	*Gillenia trifoliata*	AGM	Perennial
	Strawberry foxglove	*Digitalis* × *mertonensis*	AGM, PFP	Perennial
	Hydrangea Pink Annabelle	*Hydrangea arborescens* Pink Annabelle ('Ncha1')		Shrub
29	Panicled hydrangea 'Limelight'	*Hydrangea paniculata* 'Limelight'	AGM	Shrub
	Giant hyssop 'Blackadder'	*Agastache* 'Blackadder'	PFP	Perennial
30	Red-hot poker 'Tawny King'	*Kniphofia* 'Tawny King'	AGM	Perennial
	Pheasant's tail grass	*Anemanthele lessoniana*	AGM	Grass
	Marsh spurge	*Euphorbia palustris*	AGM, PFP	Perennial
	Foxglove 'Firecracker'	*Digitalis* × *valinii* 'Firecracker'		Perennial
31	Yarrow 'Terracotta'	*Achillea* 'Terracotta'	PFP	Perennial
	Wand loosestrife 'Dropmore Purple'	*Lythrum virgatum* 'Dropmore Purple'	PFP	Perennial
32	Mexican fleabane 'Lavender Lady'	*Erigeron karvinskianus* 'Lavender Lady'	PFP	Perennial
	Catmint 'Dawn to Dusk'	*Nepeta grandiflora* 'Dawn to Dusk'	PFP	Perennial
	Oriental fountain grass 'Karley Rose'	*Pennisetum orientale* 'Karley Rose'		Grass
	Cosmea 'Candy Stripe'	*Cosmos bipinnatus* 'Candy Stripe'	PFP	Annual
33	Pale purple coneflower	*Echinacea pallida*		Perennial
	Mexican feather grass	*Stipa tenuissima*	AGM	Perennial
	Gaura 'Whirling Butterflies'	*Oenothera lindheimeri* 'Whirling Butterflies'	PFP	Perennial
34	Eulalia 'Ferner Osten'	*Miscanthus sinensis* 'Ferner Osten'	AGM	Grass
	Rooper's red-hot poker	*Kniphofia rooperi*	AGM	Perennial
	Montbretia 'Lucifer'	*Crocosmia* 'Lucifer'	AGM	Perennial
35	Rosemary Prostrata Group	*Salvia rosmarinus* Prostrata Group	PFP	Shrub
	Mexican feather grass	*Stipa tenuissima*	AGM	Grass
	African lily 'Lapis'	*Agapanthus* 'Lapis'		Perennial
	Delavay osmanthus	*Osmanthus delavayi*	AGM	Shrub
	Rosemary	*Salvia rosmarinus*	PFP	Shrub
	Silverbush	*Convolvulus cneorum*	AGM	Shrub
	Thyme Coccineus Group	*Thymus* Coccineus Group	AGM, PFP	Perennial
36	Sweetshrub 'Aphrodite'	*Calycanthus* 'Aphrodite'		Shrub
	Japanese forest grass	*Hakonechloa macra*	AGM	Grass
	Penstemon 'Pensham Plum Jerkum'	*Penstemon* 'Pensham Plum Jerkum' (Pensham Series)	PFP	Perennial

Height	Spread	Soil	Soil pH	Position	Exposure	Hardiness
1.5–2.5m (5–8ft)	0.1–0.5m (4–20in)	Chalk, loam, sand	Any	Full sun	Exposed or sheltered	H4
0.5–1m (20–39in)	0.5–1m (20–39in)	Clay, loam, sand	Acid or neutral	Full sun or partial shade	Exposed or sheltered	H7
1.5–2.5m (5–8ft)	0.1–0.5m (4–20in)	Any	Any	Full sun or partial shade	Sheltered	H3
1.5–2.5m (5–8ft)	0.1–0.5m (4–20in)	Clay, loam, sand	Any	Full sun or partial shade	Exposed or sheltered	H3
1–1.5m (3–5ft)	0.5–1m (20–39in)	Any	Any	Full sun or partial shade	Sheltered	H3
0.5–1m (20–39in)	0.1–0.5m (4–20in)	Any	Any	Full sun	Sheltered	H3
0.5–1m (20–39in)	0.1–0.5m (4–20in)	Any	Any	Full sun	Sheltered	H3
0.5–1m (20–39in)	0.1–0.5m (4–20in)	Clay, loam, sand	Acid or neutral	Partial shade	Sheltered	H7
0.5–1m (20–39in)	0.1–0.5m (4–20in)	Any	Any	Any	Exposed or sheltered	H5
1–1.5m (3–5ft)	1–1.5m (3–5ft)	Clay, loam, sand	Acid or neutral	Full sun or partial shade	Exposed or sheltered	H6
1.5–2.5m (5–8ft)	1.5–2.5m (5–8ft)	Clay, loam, sand	Any	Full sun or partial shade	Exposed or sheltered	H5
0.5–1m (20–39in)	0.1–0.5m (4–20in)	Chalk, loam, sand	Any	Full sun	Sheltered	H4
1–1.5m (3–5ft)	0.5–1m (20–39in)	Loam, sand	Acid or neutral	Full sun	Exposed	H5
0.5–1m (20–39in)	1–1.5m (3–5ft)	Any	Any	Full sun or partial shade	Exposed or sheltered	H4
0.5–1m (20–39in)	0.5–1m (20–39in)	Clay, loam	Any	Full sun	Exposed or sheltered	H7
0.5–1m (20–39in)	0.1–0.5m (4–20in)	Any	Any	Full sun or partial shade	Exposed or sheltered	H4
1–1.5m (3–5ft)	0.1–0.5m (4–20in)	Chalk, loam, sand	Any	Full sun	Exposed	H7
1–1.5m (3–5ft)	0.1–0.5m (4–20in)	Clay, loam	Any	Full sun	Exposed or sheltered	H6
0.1–0.5m (4–20in)	0.5–1m (20–39in)	Any	Any	Full sun	Exposed	H5
0.5–1m (20–39in)	0.1–0.5m (4–20in)	Chalk, loam, sand	Any	Full sun	Exposed or sheltered	H6
0.5–1m (20–39in)	0.5–1m (20–39in)	Chalk, loam, sand	Any	Full sun	Sheltered	H3
1–1.5m (3–5ft)	0.5–1m (20–39in)	Any	Any	Full sun	Sheltered	H3
1–1.5m (3–5ft)	0.1–0.5m (4–20in)	Chalk, loam, sand	Any	Full sun	Exposed or sheltered	H5
0.5–1m (20–39in)	0.1–0.5m (4–20in)	Any	Any	Full sun	Exposed or sheltered	H4
0.5–1m (20–39in)	0.1–0.5m (4–20in)	Chalk, loam, sand	Any	Full sun or partial shade	Exposed or sheltered	H4
1–1.5m (3–5ft)	0.5–1m (20–39in)	Any	Any	Full sun	Exposed or sheltered	H6
1–1.5m (3–5ft)	0.5–1m (20–39in)	Loam, sand	Acid or neutral	Full sun	Exposed or sheltered	H5
1.5–2.5m (5–8ft)	0.1–0.5m (4–20in)	Any	Any	Full sun or partial shade	Exposed or sheltered	H5
0.1–0.5m (4–20in)	1–1.5m (3–5ft)	Chalk, loam, sand	Any	Full sun	Sheltered	H4
0.5–1m (20–39in)	0.1–0.5m (4–20in)	Any	Any	Full sun	Exposed or sheltered	H4
0.5–1m (20–39in)	0.1–0.5m (4–20in)	Chalk, loam, sand	Any	Full sun	Sheltered	H4
2.5–4m (8–13ft)	2.5–4m (8–13ft)	Any	Any	Full sun or partial shade	Exposed or sheltered	H5
1.5–2.5m (5–8ft)	1.5–2.5m (5–8ft)	Chalk, loam, sand	Any	Full sun	Sheltered	H4
0.5–1m (20–39in)	0.5–1m (20–39in)	Chalk, loam, sand	Any	Full sun	Sheltered	H4
Up to 10cm (4in)	0.1–0.5m (4–20in)	Chalk, loam, sand	Alkaline or neutral	Full sun	Exposed	H5
2.5–4m (8–13ft)	2.5–4m (8–13ft)	Any	Any	Full sun or partial shade	Sheltered	H5
0.1–0.5m (4–20in)	0.1–0.5m (4–20in)	Any	Any	Any	Exposed or sheltered	H7
0.5–1m (20–39in)	0.1–0.5m (4–20in)	Chalk, loam, sand	Any	Full sun or partial shade	Exposed or sheltered	H4

Combination	Ingredients (Common Name)	Ingredients (Latin Name)	Awards	Plant Type
37	Purple top Sea holly Big Blue Balkan clary 'Caradonna'	*Verbena bonariensis* *Eryngium × zabelii* Big Blue ('Myersblue') *Salvia nemorosa* 'Caradonna'	AGM, PFP AGM AGM, PFP	Perennial Perennial Perennial
38	Coneflower 'Goldsturm' Eulalia 'Ferner Osten'	*Rudbeckia fulgida* var. *sullivantii* 'Goldsturm' *Miscanthus sinensis* 'Ferner Osten'	AGM, PFP AGM	Perennial Grass
39	Spiny bear's breech Japanese anemone 'Andrea Atkinson' Chinese fountain grass 'Hameln'	*Acanthus spinosus* *Anemone × hybrida* 'Andrea Atkinson' *Pennisetum alopecuroides* 'Hameln'	 AGM	Perennial Perennial Grass
40	Eulalia 'Gracillimus' Culver's root 'Fascination'	*Miscanthus sinensis* 'Gracillimus' *Veronicastrum virginicum* 'Fascination'	 PFP	Grass Perennial
41	Tufted hair grass Sage 'Amistad'	*Deschampsia cespitosa* *Salvia* 'Amistad'	 AGM, PFP	Grass Perennial
42	Culver's root 'Album' Coneflower 'Alba' Chinese fountain grass	*Veronicastrum virginicum* 'Album' *Echinacea purpurea* 'Alba' *Pennisetum alopecuroides*	AGM, PFP PFP 	Perennial Perennial Grass
43	Salvia Amistad Milky bellflower 'Prichard's Variety'	*Salvia* 'Amistad' *Campanula lactiflora* 'Prichard's Variety'	AGM, PFP AGM, PFP	Perennial Perennial
44	Balkan clary 'Caradonna' English lavender Giant hyssop	*Salvia nemorosa* 'Caradonna' *Lavandula angustifolia* *Agastache* 'Blue Fortune'	AGM, PFP PFP AGM, PFP	Perennial Perennial Perennial
45	Sneezeweed 'Moerheim Beauty' Eulalia 'Red Chief'	*Helenium* 'Moerheim Beauty' *Miscanthus sinensis* 'Red Chief'	AGM, PFP 	Perennial Grass
46	Burnet 'Blackthorn' Purple moor-grass	*Sanguisorba* 'Blackthorn' *Molinia caerulea*		Perennial Grass
47	Pheasant's tail grass Winged spindle	*Anemanthele lessoniana* *Euonymus alatus*	AGM 	Grass Shrub
48	Narrow-leaved mock privet Silver spear Mexican feather grass	*Phillyrea angustifolia* *Astelia chathamica* *Stipa tenuissima*	 AGM AGM	Tree Perennial Grass
49	Flowering dogwood red-form Ivy-leaved cyclamen White-flowered ivy-leaved cyclamen Palm sedge	*Cornus florida* f. *rubra* *Cyclamen hederifolium* *Cyclamen hederifolium* var. *hederifolium* f. *albiflorum* *Carex muskingumensis*	 AGM AGM 	Tree Perennial Perennial Grass
50	Strawberry tree Tufted hair grass Switch grass 'Rehbraun'	*Arbutus unedo* *Deschampsia cespitosa* *Panicum virgatum* 'Rehbraun'	PFP 	Tree Grass Grass

Height	Spread	Soil	Soil pH	Position	Exposure	Hardiness
1.5–2.5m (5–8ft)	0.1–0.5m (4–20in)	Chalk, loam, sand	Any	Full sun	Exposed or sheltered	H4
0.5–1m (20–39in)	0.1–0.5m (4–20in)	Chalk, loam, sand	Any	Full sun	Exposed or sheltered	H5
0.1–0.5m (4–20in)	0.1–0.5m (4–20in)	Chalk, loam, sand	Any	Full sun or partial shade	Exposed or sheltered	H7
0.5–1m (20–39in)	0.1–0.5m (4–20in)	Chalk, clay, loam	Any	Full sun or partial shade	Exposed or sheltered	H6
1–1.5m (3–5ft)	0.5–1m (20–39in)	Any	Any	Full sun	Exposed or sheltered	H6
1–1.5m (3–5ft)	0.5–1m (20–39in)	Any	Any	Full sun or partial shade	Exposed or sheltered	H5
0.5–1m (20–39in)	0.5–1m (20–39in)	Any	Any	Full sun or partial shade	Exposed or sheltered	H6
0.5–1m (20–39in)	0.5–1m (20–39in)	Chalk, loam, sand	Any	Full sun	Sheltered	H3
1–1.8m (3–6ft)	0.5–1m (20–39in)	Any	Any	Full sun	Exposed or sheltered	H6
1–1.5m (3–5ft)	0.5–1m (20–39in)	Clay, loam	Any	Full sun or partial shade	Exposed	H7
1–1.5m (3–5ft)	0.5–1m (20–39in)	Clay, loam, sand	Acid or neutral	Full sun or partial shade	Exposed or sheltered	H6
1–1.5m (3–5ft)	0.1–0.5m (4–20in)	Chalk, loam, sand	Any	Full sun	Sheltered	H3
1–1.5m (3–5ft)	0.5–1m (20–39in)	Clay, loam	Any	Full shade or partial shade	Exposed or sheltered	H7
1–1.5m (3–5ft)	0.1–0.5m (4–20in)	Chalk, loam, sand	Any	Full sun	Exposed or sheltered	H5
1–1.5m (3–5ft)	1–1.5m (3–5ft)	Chalk, loam, sand	Any	Full sun	Sheltered	H3
1–1.5m (3–5ft)	0.1–0.5m (4–20in)	Chalk, loam, sand	Any	Full sun	Sheltered	H3
0.5–1m (20–39in)	0.1–0.5m (4–20in)	Chalk, loam	Alkaline or neutral	Full sun or partial shade	Sheltered	H7
0.1–0.5m (4–20in)	0.1–0.5m (4–20in)	Chalk, loam, sand	Any	Full sun or partial shade	Exposed or sheltered	H7
0.5–1m (20–39in)	1–1.5m (3–5ft)	Chalk, loam, sand	Any	Full sun	Sheltered	H5
0.5–1m (20–39in)	0.1–0.5m (4–20in)	Any	Any	Full sun	Exposed or sheltered	H6
0.5–1m (20–39in)	0.1–0.5m (4–20in)	Any	Any	Full sun	Exposed or sheltered	H7
1–1.5m (3–5ft)	0.5–1m (20–39in)	Any	Any	Full sun	Exposed or sheltered	H6
1–1.5m (3–5ft)	0.1–0.5m (4–20in)	Any	Any	Full sun or partial shade	Exposed or sheltered	H7
0.5–1m (20–39in)	0.5–1m (20–39in)	Clay, loam, sand	Acid or neutral	Full sun or partial shade	Exposed or sheltered	H7
0.5–1m (20–39in)	1–1.5m (3–5ft)	Any	Any	Full sun or partial shade	Exposed or sheltered	H4
0.5–1m (20–39in)	1–1.5m (3–5ft)	Any	Any	Full sun or partial shade	Exposed or sheltered	H6
2.5–4m (8–13ft)	1.5–2.5m (5–8ft)	Sand	Any	Full sun or partial shade	Exposed or sheltered	H5
1–1.5m (3–5ft)	0.5–1m (20–39in)	Clay, loam	Any	Full sun or partial shade	Sheltered	H3
0.5–1m (20–39in)	0.1–0.5m (4–20in)	Any	Any	Full sun	Exposed or sheltered	H4
4–8m (13–26ft)	4–8m (13–26ft)	Clay, loam, sand	Acid or neutral	Full sun or partial shade	Exposed or sheltered	H5
Up to 10cm (4in)	0.1–0.5m (4–20in)	Any	Any	Partial shade	Sheltered	H5
Up to 10cm (4in)	0.1–0.5m (4–20in)	Any	Any	Partial shade	Sheltered	H5
0.5–1m (20–39in)	0.5–1m (20–39in)	Any	Any	Full sun or partial shade	Exposed or sheltered	H4
4–8m (13–26ft)	4–8m (13–26ft)	Chalk, loam, sand	Any	Full sun	Sheltered	H5
1–1.5m (3–5ft)	0.5–1m (20–39in)	Clay, loam, sand	Acid or neutral	Full sun or partial shade	Exposed or sheltered	H6
1.5–2.5m (5–8ft)	0.5–1m (20–39in)	Chalk, loam, sand	Any	Full sun	Exposed or sheltered	H5

Combination	Ingredients (Common Name)	Ingredients (Latin Name)	Awards	Plant Type
51	Coneflower 'Herbstsonne' Eulalia 'Ferner Osten'	*Rudbeckia laciniata* 'Herbstsonne' *Miscanthus sinensis* 'Ferner Osten'	AGM, PFP AGM	Perennial Grass
52	Seven son flower tree Michaelmas daisy 'White Ladies' Switch grass 'Rehbraun'	*Heptacodium miconioides* *Symphyotrichum novi-belgii* 'White Ladies' *Panicum virgatum* 'Rehbraun'	AGM	Tree Perennial Grass
53	Fountain grass 'Rubrum' Oak-leaved hydrangea Chinese fountain grass 'Hameln'	*Pennisetum advena* 'Rubrum' *Hydrangea quercifolia* *Pennisetum alopecuroides* 'Hameln'	AGM AGM	Grass Shrub Grass
54	Beautyberry 'Profusion' Garden privet Field maple Switch grass 'Prairie Sky'	*Callicarpa bodinieri* var. *giraldii* 'Profusion' *Ligustrum ovalifolium* *Acer campestre* *Panicum virgatum* 'Prairie Sky'	AGM, PFP PFP PFP	Shrub Shrub Shrub Grass
55	Common medlar Switch grass 'Northwind' Alpine strawberry	*Mespilus germanica* *Panicum virgatum* 'Northwind' *Fragaria vesca*	PFP AGM PFP	Tree Grass Perennial
56	Stag's horn sumach Orange New Zealand sedge	*Rhus typhina* *Carex testacea*		Tree Grass
57	Purple moor-grass 'Moorhexe' Coneflower 'Goldsturm' Maidenhair tree 'Globus'	*Molinia caerulea* subsp. *caerulea* 'Moorhexe' *Rudbeckia fulgida* var. *sullivantii* 'Goldsturm' *Ginkgo biloba* 'Globus'	AGM AGM, PFP AGM	Grass Perennial Tree
58	Japanese aralia Necklace vine Canna 'Cleopatra' Canna 'Durban'	*Fatsia japonica* *Muehlenbeckia complexa* *Canna* 'Cleopatra' AGM *Canna* 'Durban'	AGM, PFP AGM	Shrub Perennial Perennial Perennial
59	Japanese maple 'Dissectum' Japanese forest grass	*Acer palmatum* 'Dissectum' *Hakonechloa macra*	 AGM	Tree Grass
60	Chinese fountain grass 'Hameln' White wood aster	*Pennisetum alopecuroides* 'Hameln' *Eurybia divaricata*	AGM	Grass Perennial
61	West Himalayan birch Scaly male fern Tree ivy	*Betula utilis* subsp. *jacquemontii* *Dryopteris affinis* *Hedera helix* 'Arborescens'	AGM PFP	Tree Fern Shrub
62	Paperbark maple Common rasp-fern Heavenly bamboo	*Acer griseum* *Doodia media* *Nandina domestica* Obsessed ('Seika')	AGM	Tree Fern Shrub
63	Winter-flowering cherry 'Autumnalis' Heucherella 'Sweet Tea' Orange New Zealand sedge	*Prunus* × *subhirtella* 'Autumnalis' × *Heucherella* 'Sweet Tea' *Carex testacea*		Tree Perennial Grass
64	Common yew Japanese forest grass Mexican fleabane	*Taxus baccata* *Hakonechloa macra* *Erigeron karvinskianus*	AGM AGM AGM, PFP	Topiary Grass Perennial

Height	Spread	Soil	Soil pH	Position	Exposure	Hardiness
1.5–2.5m (5–8ft)	0.5–1m (20–39in)	Chalk, clay, loam	Any	Full sun or partial shade	Exposed or sheltered	H6
1–1.5m (3–5ft)	0.5–1m (20–39in)	Any	Any	Full sun	Exposed or sheltered	H6
4–8m (13–26ft)	2.5–4m (8–13ft)	Any	Any	Full sun or partial shade	Sheltered	H7
0.5–1m (20–39in)	0.1–0.5m (4–20in)	Any	Any	Full sun or partial shade	Exposed or sheltered	H6
1.5–2.5m (5–8ft)	0.5–1m (20–39in)	Chalk, loam, sand	Any	Full sun	Exposed or sheltered	H5
1–1.5m (3–5ft)	0.5–1m (20–39in)	Loam, sand	Any	Full sun	Sheltered	H3
1–1.5m (3–5ft)	1.5–2.5m (5–8ft)	Clay, loam, sand	Acid or neutral	Full sun or partial shade	Exposed or sheltered	H5
0.5–1m (20–39in)	0.5–1m (20–39in)	Chalk, loam, sand	Any	Full sun	Sheltered	H3
2.5–4m (8–13ft)	1.5–2.5m (5–8ft)	Any	Any	Full sun or partial shade	Exposed or sheltered	H6
4–8m (13–26ft)	2.5–4m (8–13ft)	Any	Any	Full sun	Exposed or sheltered	H4
Over 12m (39ft)	4–8m (13–26ft)	Any	Neutral	Full sun or partial shade	Exposed	H6
1–1.5m (3–5ft)	0.5–1m (20–39in)	Any	Any	Full sun	Exposed or sheltered	H5
4–8m (13–26ft)	4–8m (13–26ft)	Any	Any	Full sun or partial shade	Full sun or partial shade	H6
1–1.5m (3–5ft)	0.5–1m (20–39in)	Chalk, loam, sand	Any	Full sun	Full sun	H5
0.1–0.5m (4–20in)	0.5–1m (20–39in)	Clay, loam, sand	Any	Full sun	Full sun	H6
4–8m (13–26ft)	4–8m (13–26ft)	Any	Any	Full sun	Exposed or sheltered	H6
0.5–1m (20–39in)	0.5–1m (20–39in)	Any	Any	Full sun or partial shade	Sheltered	H5
0.1–0.5m (4–20in)	0.1–0.5m (4–20in)	Any	Acid or neutral	Full sun or partial shade	Exposed or sheltered	H7
0.5–1m (20–39in)	0.1–0.5m (4–20in)	Chalk, clay, loam	Any	Full sun or partial shade	Exposed or sheltered	H6
4m (13ft)	1.5m (5ft)	Any	Any	Full sun or partial shade	Exposed or sheltered	H6
2.5–4m (8–13ft)	2.5–4m (8–13ft)	Any	Any	Any	Sheltered	H5
2.5–4m (8–13ft)	1.5–2.5m (5–8ft)	Chalk, loam, sand	Any	Full sun or partial shade	Sheltered	H3
1–1.5m (3–5ft)	0.5–1m (20–39in)	Loam, sand	Any	Full sun	Sheltered	H3
1.5–2.5m (5–8ft)	0.5–1m (20–39in)	Loam, sand	Any	Full sun	Sheltered	H3
1.5–2.5m (5–8ft)	1.5–2.5m (5–8ft)	Any	Acid or neutral	Full sun or partial shade	Sheltered	H6
0.1–0.5m (4–20in)	0.1–0.5m (4–20in)	Any	Any	Any	Exposed or sheltered	H7
0.5–1m (20–39in)	0.5–1m (20–39in)	Chalk, loam, sand	Any	Full sun	Sheltered	H3
0.5–1m (20–39in)	0.5–1m (20–39in)	Clay, loam, sand	Any	Full sun or partial shade	Exposed or sheltered	H7
Over 12m (39ft)	4–8m (13–26ft)	Any	Any	Full sun or partial shade	Exposed or sheltered	H7
1–1.5m (3–5ft)	0.5–1m (20–39in)	Any	Any	Any	Exposed or sheltered	H5
0.5–1m (20–39in)	0.5–1m (20–39in)	Any	Any	Any	Exposed or sheltered	H5
8–12m (26–39ft)	4–8m (13–26ft)	Any	Any	Full sun or partial shade	Sheltered	H5
0.1–0.5m (4–20in)	0.5–1m (20–39in)	Loam	Acid	Partial shade	Sheltered	H3
0.5–1m (20–39in)	0.5–1m (20–39in)	Any	Any	Full sun	Sheltered	H5
4–8m (13–26ft)	4–8m (13–26ft)	Any	Any	Full sun	Exposed or sheltered	H6
0.1–0.5m (4–20in)	0.1–0.5m (4–20in)	Loam, sand	Neutral	Full sun or partial shade	Exposed or sheltered	H6
0.5–1m (20–39in)	0.5–1m (20–39in)	Any	Any	Full sun or partial shade	Sheltered	H5
Over 12m (39ft)	Over 8m (26ft)	Any	Any	Any	Exposed or sheltered	H7
0.1–0.5m (4–20in)	0.1–0.5m (4–20in)	Any	Any	Any	Exposed or sheltered	H7
0.1–0.5m (4–20in)	0.1–0.5m (4–20in)	Any	Any	Full sun	Exposed	H5

RESOURCES

RHS www.rhs.org.uk

RHS Plant Finder, for plant referencing and nomenclature www.rhs.org.uk/plants/search-form

RHS Propagating Plants, edited by Alan Toogood (DK, 2025)

INDEX

A

Acanthus
   A. mollis 60–61
   A. spinosus 130–33
Acer
   A. campestre 174–75
   A. griseum 30–31, 194–95
   A. palmatum 'Dissectum' 186–87
Achillea 24
   A. millefolium 'Lilac Beauty' 78–79
   A. 'Moonshine' 68–69
   A. 'Terracotta' 108–109
African lily 'Lapis' 118–21
Agapanthus 39
   A. 'Lapis' 118–21
Agastache
   A. 'Blackadder' 102–103
   A. 'Blue Fortune' 146–47
AGM (Award of Garden Merit) 15
Alchemilla mollis 80–83
Allium 24, 108, 115
   A. 'Graceful Beauty' 84–85
   A. 'Mont Blanc' 72–73, 136
   A. 'Red Mohican' 156
   A. stipitatum 'Mount Everest' 46–47
alpine strawberry 176–77
alpine wood fern 48–49
Anemanthele lessoniana 46–47, 104–107, 156–57

Anemone 24
   A. × *hybrida* 'Andrea Atkinson' 130–33
   A. × *h.* 'Whirlwind' 90–91
   A. REGAL SWAN 84–85
annuals 13, 16
Aquilegia vulgaris 48–49
aralia Green Fingers 58–59
Arbutus unedo 164–65
Aruncus 'Horatio' 54–55
Astella chathamica 158–59
Autumn 154–99
avens 'Prinses Juliana' 32–35

B

Balkan clary 'Caradonna' 42–45, 124–27, 146–47
ball-like flower heads 24
Baltic parsley 60–61
barrenwort
   large-flowered barrenwort 30–31
bearded iris 38–39
bear's breech 60–61
beautyberry 'Profusion' 174–75
bee's primrose 54–55
bellflower
   milky bellflower 'Prichard's Variety' 142–45
Betula utilis subsp. *jacquemontii* 190–93
birch 62
   west Himalayan birch 190–93
bistort
   red bistort 'Superba' 84–85
Bistorta officinalis 'Superba' 84–85
Blechnum spicant 40–41, 58–59, 74–75
bloody cranesbill 'Album' 50–53
blue eryngo 92–95
bowman's root 98–101
bronze fennel 42–45, 86–89
bulbs 13, 16
   see also individual species
burnet 'Blackthorn' 152–53

C

Callicarpa bodinieri var. *giraldii* 'Profusion' 174–75
Calycanthus 'Aphrodite' 122–23
Campanula lactiflora 'Prichard's Variety' 142–45
Canna
   C. 'Cleopatra' 184–85
   C. 'Durban' 184–85
Cappadocian navelwort 'Cherry Ingram' 58–59
Carex
   C. muskingumensis 160–63
   C. testacea 178–79, 196–97
catmint
   'Dawn to Dusk' 110–11
   'Purrsian Blue' 42–45
   'Six Hills Giant' 80–83
   'Summer Magic' 68–69
Cenolophium 24
   C. denudatum 60–61
Cercis 59
cherry
   winter-flowering cherry 'Autumnalis' 196–97
Chinese dogwood 64–67
Chinese fountain grass 138–41
   'Hameln' 90–91, 130–33, 170–73, 188–89
Choisya × *dewitteana* 'Aztec Pearl' 104
choosing plants 16
Cirsium rivulare 'Atropurpureum' 40–41
clusters, flower 24, 25
colour 21, 22
columbine, common 48–49
combinations, designing 20–25
common columbine 48–49
common medlar 176–77
common myrtle 124
common rasp-fern 194–95
common yew 198–99
compost 10–11

coneflowers
  'Alba' 138–41
  'Goldsturm' 128–29, 180–83
  'Herbstsonne' 166–67
  pale purple coneflower 112–15
containers 11
Convallaria majalis 58–59
Convolvulus cneorum 118–21
copper shield fern 30–31, 48–49, 70–71
  'Brilliance' 64–67
Cornus
  C. florida f. *rubra* 160–63
  C. kousa var. *chinensis* 64–67
  C. sanguinea 'Midwinter Fire' 104
Corylus avellana 48–49
cosmea
  'Apricotta' 96–97
  'Candy Stripe' 110–11
  'Purity' 96–97
  'Rubenza' 96–97
Cosmos 24, 37
  C. bipinnatus 'Apricotta' 96–97
  C. b. 'Candy Stripe' 110–11
  C. b. 'Purity' 96–97
  C. b. 'Rubenza' 96–97
Cotinus coggygria 'Royal Purple' 104
cranesbill
  bloody cranesbill 'Album' 50–53
  dusky cranesbill 40–41
  dusky cranesbill 'Lily Lovell' 48–49
Crocosmia 'Lucifer' 86–89, 116–17
Culver's root
  'Album' 138–41
  'Fascination' 134–35
cup-shaped flowers 24
cutting back 18
cutting tools 10
Cyclamen
  C. hederifolium 160–63
  C. h. var. *hederifolium* f. *albiflorum* 160–63

D
daffodils 13, 24, 115, 160
daisies 24
deadheading 18
delavay osmanthus 46–47, 118–21
Deschampsia cespitosa 136–37, 164–65
designing combinations 20–25
Digitalis
  D. purpurea 'Sutton's Apricot' 60–61
  D. × *mertonensis* 98–101
  D. × *valinii* 'Firecracker' 104–107
dividing plants 18–19
dogwood
  Chinese dogwood 64–67
  flowering dogwood red-form 160–63
Doodia media 194–95
Dryopteris
  D. affinis 190–93
  D. cycadina 64–67
  D. erythrosora 30–31, 48–49, 70–71
  D. e. 'Brilliance' 64–67
  D. filix-mas 30–31, 40–41, 54–55
  D. wallichiana 48–49
dusky cranesbill 40–41
  'Lily Lovell' 48–49
dwarf mountain pine 124

E
Echinacea
  E. pallida 112–15
  E. purpurea 'Alba' 138–41
English lavender 146–47
Enkianthus campanulatus 40–41
Epimedium grandiflorum 30–31
equipment 10–11
Erigeron 24, 39
  E. karvinskianus 36–37, 198–99
  E. k. 'Lavender Lady' 110–11

Eryngium
  E. planum 92–95
  E. × *zabelii* Big Blue 124–27
eulalia
  'Ferner Osten' 116–17, 128–29, 166–67
  'Gracillimus' 72–73, 134–35
  'Red Chief' 148–51
Euonymus alatus 156–57
Euphorbia 24
  E. amygdaloides var. *robbiae* 30–31
  E. characias 'Black Pearl' 32–35
  E. c. subsp. *wulfenii* 36–37
  E. palustris 60–61, 104–107
Eurybia divaricata 46–47, 188–89

F
Fatsia
  F. japonica 184–85
  F. polycarpa Green Fingers 58–59
Feijoa sellowiana 36–37
fennel 24
  bronze fennel 42–45, 86–89
ferns 30–31
  alpine wood fern 48–49
  common rasp-fern 194–95
  copper shield fern 30–31, 48–49, 70–71
  copper shield fern 'Brilliance' 64–67
  hard fern 40–41, 58–59, 74–75
  male fern 40–41, 54–55
  scaly male fern 190–93
  soft shield fern 64–67
  soft shield fern 'Herrenhausen' 70–71
fertilizer 11
field maple 174–75
filler plants 24
flat tops 24
fleabane, Mexican 198–99
flowering dogwood red-form 160–63

flowers, shape and habit 24–25
Foeniculum vulgare 'Purpureum' 42–45, 86–89
foliage 18, 21, 22
form 25
fountain grass
    Chinese fountain grass 138–41
    Chinese fountain grass 'Hameln' 90–91, 130–33, 170–73, 188–89
    fountain grass 'Rubrum' 170–73
    oriental fountain grass 'Karley Rose' 110–11
foxgloves 24
    'Firecracker' 104–107
    strawberry foxglove 98–101
    'Sutton's Apricot' 60–61
Fragaria vesca 176–77
frost 18

G

garden catmint 'Purrsian Blue' 42–45
garden privet 174–75
gaura 'Whirling Butterflies' 112–15
Geranium
    G. phaeum 40–41
    G. p. 'Lily Lovell' 48–49
    G. 'Rozanne' 102
    G. sanguineum 'Album' 50–53
Geum 'Prinses Juliana' 32–35
giant blue hosta 50–53
giant hyssop 146–47
    'Blackadder' 102–103
Gillenia trifoliata 98–101
Ginkgo biloba 'Globus' 180–83
globe-shaped flowers 24
goat's beard 'Horatio' 54–55
grasses 13, 21, 22, 25
    see also individual species

H

Hakonechloa macra 122–23, 186–87, 198–99
Hamamelis 59
hard fern 40–41, 58–59, 74–75
hazel 48–49, 62
heavenly bamboo 194–95
Hedera helix 'Arborescens' 190–93
Helenium 'Moerheim Beauty' 148–51
Heptacodium miconioides 168–69
herbaceous perennials 13
× *Heucherella* 'Sweet Tea' 196–97
Hosta
    H. 'Devon Green' 50–53, 74–75
    H. 'Krossa Regal' 50–53, 74–75
    H. sieboldiana var. *elegans* 50–53
Hydrangea
    H. arborescens PINK ANNABELLE 98–101
    H. a. STRONG ANNABELLE 80–83
    H. paniculata 'Limelight' 102–103
    H. quercifolia 170–73
hyssop
    giant hyssop 146–47
    giant hyssop 'Blackadder' 102–103

I

Iris
    I. 'Caesar's Brother' 70–71
    I. 'Kent Pride' 36–37
    I. 'Sable Night' 38–39
ivy, tree 190–93
ivy-leaved cyclamen 160–63

J

Japanese anemone
    'Andrea Atkinson' 130–33
    'Whirlwind' 90–91
Japanese aralia 184–85
Japanese forest grass 122–23, 186–87, 198–99
Japanese maple 'Dissectum' 186–87
Japanese primrose 'Alba' 54–55, 74–75

K

Knautia macedonica 72–73
Kniphofia
    K. rooperi 116–17
    K. 'Tawny King' 104–107

L

lady's mantle 80–83
large-flowered barrenwort 30–31
Lathyrus odoratus
    'Black Knight' 96–97
    'Mrs Collier' 96–97
Lavandula angustifolia 146–47
lavender, English 146–47
Leucojum aestivum 'Gravetye Giant' 30–31
lifespans of plants 19
Ligustrum ovalifolium 174–75
lilies 24
lily of the valley 58–59
Lobelia × *speciosa* 'Hadspen Purple' 78–79
locations, planting 8
loosestrife
    purple loosestrife 'Feuerkerze' 78–79
    wand loosestrife 'Dropmore Purple' 108–109
loppers 10
Luzula nivea 32–35
Lythrum
    L. salicaria 'Feuerkerze' 78–79
    L. virgatum 'Dropmore Purple' 108–109

M

Macedonian scabious 72–73
maidenhair tree 'Globus' 180–83
male fern 40–41, 54–55
maple
    field maple 174–75
    Japanese maple 'Dissectum' 186–87
    paperbark maple 194–95

marsh spurge 60–61, 104–107
materials 10–11
meadow rue 'Black Stockings' 32–35
Mediterranean spurge 36–37
medlar, common 176–77
Melica altissima 'Atropurpurea' 28–29
Mespilus germanica 176–77
Mexican feather grass 36–37, 38–39, 112–15, 118–21, 158–59
Mexican fleabane 36–37, 198–99
  'Lavender Lady' 110–11
Michaelmas daisy 'White Ladies' 168–69
mildew 72
milky bellflower 'Prichard's Variety' 142–45
Miscanthus sinensis
  'Ferner Osten' 116–17, 128–29, 166–67
  'Gracillimus' 72–73, 134–35
  'Red Chief' 148–51
Mrs Robb's bonnet 30–31
Molinia 78
  M. caerulea 96–97, 152–53
  M. c. subsp. *caerulea* 'Heidebraut' 84–85, 86–87
  M. c. subsp. *c.* 'Moorhexe' 180–83
  M. c. subsp. *c.* 'Poul Petersen' 56–57
montbretia 'Lucifer' 86–89, 116–17
moor-grass
  purple moor-grass 56–57, 96–97, 152–53
  purple moor-grass 'Heidebraut' 84–85, 86–87
  purple moor-grass 'Moorhexe' 180–83
mountain pine, dwarf 124
Muehlenbeckia complexa 184–85
myrtle, common 124
Myrtus communis 124

N

Nandina domestica OBSESSED 194–95
Narcissus 13, 24, 115, 160
  N. 'Pheasant's Eye' 160
  N. 'Thalia' 136, 160
narrow-leaved mock privet 56–57, 158–59
necklace vine 184–85
Nepeta 24
  N. × *faassenii* 'Purrsian Blue' 42–45
  N. grandiflora 'Dawn to Dusk' 110–11
  N. g. 'Summer Magic' 68–69
  N. 'Little Titch' 102
  N. 'Six Hills Giant' 80–83

O

oak-leaved hydrangea 170–73
Oenothera lindheimeri 'Whirling Butterflies' 112–15
Omphalodes cappadocica 'Cherry Ingram' 58–59
orange New Zealand sedge 178–79, 196–97
oriental fountain grass 'Karley Rose' 110–11
ornamental grasses 13, 21, 22, 25
  see also individual species
Osmanthus delavayi 46–47, 118–21

P

Paeonia
  P. 'Coral Charm' 62–63
  P. lactiflora 'Sarah Bernhardt' 28–29, 62–63
pale purple coneflower 112–15
palm sedge 160–63
panicled hydrangea 'Limelight' 102–103
Panicum virgatum
  P. v. 'Northwind' 176–77
  P. v. 'Prairie Sky' 92–95, 174–75
  P. v. 'Rehbraun' 164–65, 168–69
paperbark maple 30–31, 194–95
pasqueflower
  red pasqueflower 38–39
  white pasqueflower 38–39
Pennisetum 78
  P. advena 'Rubrum' 170–73
  P. alopecuroides 138–41
  P. a. 'Hameln' 90–91, 130–33, 170–73, 188–89
  P. orientale 'Karley Rose' 110–11
Penstemon 'Pensham Plum Jerkum' 122–23
peonies 24, 28
  'Coral Charm' 62–63
  'Sarah Bernhardt' 28–29
perennials 13, 21
  dividing 19
perovskia 'Blue Spire' 92–95
PFP (Plants for Pollinators) 15
pheasant's tail grass 46–47, 104–107, 156–57
Phillyrea angustifolia 56–57, 158–59
pineapple guava 36–37
Pinus mugo 124
plantain lily
  'Devon Green' 50–53, 74–75
  'Krossa Regal' 50–53, 74–75
plants
  choosing and caring for 16–19
  designing combinations 20–25
  lifespans 19
  plant names and types 13–15
  planting 16
plug plants 13
plume thistle 'Atropurpureum' 40–41
pollinators 15, 18
  flower shape and 24
Polystichum setiferum 64–67
  P. s. 'Herrenhausen' 70–71
pots 11
primroses
  bee's primrose 54–55

Japanese primrose 'Alba' 54–55, 74–75
vial's primrose 54–55
Primula 24
   P. beesiana 54–55
   P. japonica 'Alba' 54–55, 74–75
   P. vialii 54–55
privet
   garden privet 174–75
   narrow-leaved mock privet 56–57
propagation 18–19
pruning 18
Prunus × *subhirtella* 'Autumnalis' 196–97
Pulsatilla
   P. rubra 38–39
   P. vulgaris 'Alba' 38–39
purple loosestrife 'Feuerkerze' 78–79
purple moor-grass 56–57, 96–97, 152–53
   'Heidebraut' 84–85, 86–87
   'Moorhexe' 180–83
purple top 96–97, 124–27

R

rasp-fern
   common rasp-fern 194–95
red bistort 'Superba' 84–85
red-hot poker
   Rooper's red-hot poker 116–17
   'Tawny King' 104–107
red pasqueflower 38–39
redbuds 59
redvein enkianthus 40–41
Rheum palmatum 'Atrosanguineum' 74–75
rhubarb 'Atrosanguineum' 74–75
Rhus typhina 178–79
Rooper's red-hot poker 116–17
rosemary 118–21
   Prostrata Group 118–21
Royal Horticultural Society (RHS)
   AGM (Award of Garden Merit) 15
   PFP (Plants for Pollinators) 15

Rudbeckia
   R. fulgida var. *sullivantii* 'Goldsturm' 128–29, 180–83
   R. laciniata 'Herbstsonne' 166–67

S

sage
   'Amistad' 136–37, 142–45
   Love and Wishes 28–29
   Pink Amistad 78–79
   wood sage 'Viola Klose' 68–69
Salvia
   S. 'Amistad' 136–7, 142–45
   S. 'Blue Note' 102
   S. 'Blue Spire' 92–95
   S. Love and Wishes 28–29
   S. nemorosa 'Caradonna' 42–45, 124–27, 146–47
   S. Pink Amistad 78–79
   S. rosmarinus 118–21
   S. r. Prostrata Group 118–21
   S. × *sylvestris* 'Viola Klose' 68–69
Sanguisorba
   S. 'Blackthorn' 152–53
   S. 'Cangshan Cranberry' 152
   S. menziesii 152
   S. 'Tanna' 152
saws, folding 10
scaly male fern 190–93
screens 21
sea holly Big Blue 124–27
seasonal interest 22
seaweed fertilizer 11
secateurs 10, 18
sedge
   orange New Zealand sedge 178–79, 196–97
   palm sedge 160–63
seedheads 18
seeds 13
seven son flower tree 168–69
shaggy shield fern 64–67
shears 10, 18

shield ferns
   copper shield fern 30–31, 48–49, 70–71
   copper shield fern 'Brilliance' 64–67
   shaggy shield fern 64–67
   soft shield fern 64–67
   soft shield fern 'Herrenhausen' 70–71
shrubs 14, 21
   form 25
   pruning 18
   topiary 14
Siberian iris 'Caesar's Brother' 70–71
Siberian melic 28–29
silver spear 158–59
silverbush 118–21
slugs and snails 53, 75
sneezeweed 'Moerheim Beauty' 148–51
snips 10
snow rush 32–35
soft shield fern 64–67
   'Herrenhausen' 70–71
spaces, how plants change 21
spades 10
spikes 24
spiny bear's breech 130–33
spires 24
Spring 26–75
spurge
   marsh spurge 60–61, 104–107
   spurge 'Black Pearl' 32–35
stag's horn sumach 178–79
Stipa tenuissima 36–37, 38–39, 112–15, 118–21, 158–59
strawberry
   alpine strawberry 176–77
strawberry foxglove 98–101
strawberry tree 164–65
structure, winter 18
Summer 76–153
summer snowflake 'Gravetye Giant' 30–31

sweet peas
    'Black Knight' 96–97
    'Mrs Collier' 96–97
sweetshrub 'Aphrodite' 122–23
switch grass
    'Northwind' 176–77
    'Prairie Sky' 92–95, 174–75
    'Rehbraun' 164–65, 168–69
Symphyotrichum novi-belgii
    'White Ladies' 168–69

T
Taxus baccata 198–99
Tellima grandiflora 'Forest Frost' 58–59
tetrapanax 59
texture 21, 22
Thalictrum 'Black Stockings' 32–35
thyme
    'Albiflorus' 36–37
    Coccineus Group 118–21
Thymus
    T. Coccineus Group 118–21
    T. praecox 'Albiflorus' 36–7
tools 10
topiary 14, 21
tree ivy 190–93
trees 14, 21
    choosing 16
    form 25
    planting 16
    pruning 18
    topiary 14
trowels 10
trumpets 24
tufted hair grass 136–37, 164–65
Tulipa (tulips) 24, 108, 115
    T. 'Ballerina' 116, 148, 156
    T. 'Bastogne' 116
    T. 'Bronze Charm' 148
    T. 'Disaronno' 148
    T. 'Mascara' 148
    T. 'Orange Princess' 116
    T. 'Queen of Night' 136, 196
    T. 'Spring Green' 57, 84–85, 136
    T. sylvestris 196

U
umbels 24, 25

V
Verbena 24, 37, 39
    V. bonariensis 96–97, 124–27
    V. macdougalii 'Lavender Spires' 57
Veronicastrum virginicum
    V. v. 'Album' 138–41
    V. v. 'Fascination' 134–35
vial's primrose 54–55

W
wand loosestrife 'Dropmore Purple' 108–109
water 11
west Himalayan birch 190–93
white-flowered ivy-leaved cyclamen 160–63
white pasqueflower 38–39
white wood aster 46–47, 188–89
winged spindle 156–57
winter-flowering cherry 'Autumnalis' 196–97
winter structure 18
witch hazel 59
wood sage 'Viola Klose' 68–69

Y
yarrow
    'Lilac Beauty' 78–79
    'Moonshine' 68–69
    'Terracotta' 108–109
yew
    common yew 198–99

ACKNOWLEDGMENTS

AUTHOR ACKNOWLEDGMENTS

This book would not have been possible without the support, trust, and hard work of so many people to turn what was nothing more than a dream and aspiration into the reality you're now reading.

Chris Young, for believing in this book, and everyone at DK, who put faith and confidence in my ideas: Ruth, Lucy, Barbara, and Jane, thank you so much.

Rachel Warne for your incredibly beautiful photography, impeccable taste in music, and patience while we created each set.

William, Jack, Mark, Kim, Adam, Phil, Sam, Adam, Dan, and Jake, for your help in setting up each and every one of the combinations and hard work in growing all of the plants. Form Plants, for providing all of the beautiful plants, trees, and shrubs required.

Finally to Devon, Hector, and Ollie for the endless patience, cups of tea, and supportive tail wags while I locked myself away to write this.

PUBLISHER ACKNOWLEDGMENTS

DK would like to thank Kathy Steer for proofreading, Vanessa Bird for indexing, and Adam Brackenbury for repro work.

Editorial Director Ruth O'Rourke
Project Editor Lucy Philpott
Senior Designer Barbara Zuniga
DTP and Design Co-ordinator Heather Blagden
Production Editor David Almond
Production Controller Kariss Ainsworth
Jacket and Sales Material Co-ordinator Emily Cannings
Art Director Maxine Pedliham
Publishing Director Stephanie Jackson

Editorial Jane Simmonds
Design Studio Nic+Lou
Photography Rachel Warne
Consultant Gardening Publisher Chris Young

First published in Great Britain in 2025 by
Dorling Kindersley Limited
20 Vauxhall Bridge Road,
London SW1V 2SA

The authorised representative in the EEA is
Dorling Kindersley Verlag GmbH. Arnulfstr. 124,
80636 Munich, Germany

Copyright © 2025 Dorling Kindersley Limited
A Penguin Random House Company
Text copyright © Jamie Butterworth 2025

Jamie Butterworth has asserted his right to be identified
as the author of this work.

10 9 8 7 6 5 4 3 2
004–345571–Sep/2025

All rights reserved.
No part of this publication may be reproduced, stored in or introduced into a retrieval system, or transmitted, in any form, or by any means (electronic, mechanical, photocopying, recording, or otherwise), without the prior written permission of the copyright owner.
DK values and supports copyright. Thank you for respecting intellectual property laws by not reproducing, scanning or distributing any part of this publication by any means without permission. By purchasing an authorised edition, you are supporting writers and artists and enabling DK to continue to publish books that inform and inspire readers.
No part of this publication may be used or reproduced in any manner for the purpose of training artificial intelligence technologies or systems. In accordance with Article 4(3) of the DSM Directive 2019/790, DK expressly reserves this work from the text and data mining exception.

A CIP catalogue record for this book
is available from the British Library.
ISBN: 978-0-2417-2307-4

Printed and bound in the UK

www.dk.com

This book was made with Forest Stewardship Council™ certified paper – one small step in DK's commitment to a sustainable future. Learn more at www.dk.com/uk/information/sustainability

ABOUT THE AUTHOR

Jamie Butterworth is a passionate plantsman and horticulturist. He is one of the UK's leading – and youngest – nursery owners, establishing Form Plants in 2020. He trained at RHS Garden Wisley and has since worked on more than 15 RHS Show Gardens, winning four RHS gold medals (including at the RHS Chelsea Flower Show).

Jamie has been an RHS Ambassador since the age of 24.